Literary Titan Review

★ ★ ★ ★ ★　"Simon I. Perlsweig's historical account shows a great deal of what life in Springfield, VT was like in the 1910's… It is a real pleasure to be able to experience this slice of history. Simon Perlsweig does this astoundingly and it is clearly evident that he put his heart and soul into his work. Perlsweig's book takes readers to Springfield, and more importantly, into the lives of a couple whose lives were greatly affected by WWI…

…The research is thorough, and the writing style employed by the author is academic, while at the same time being accessible to a diverse audience… Another aspect of the book that many readers should enjoy is the fact that there is a large amount of authentic memorabilia from the period, including recruiting posters, family photos, government documents, and much more… It is not every day that we are invited into the human experience of those who lived through one of America's most trying times."

Beverly Hills Book Award

Established in 2013, the Beverly Hills Book Awards competition is judged by experts from all aspects of the book industry including publishers, writers, editors, book designers and professional copywriters. Contest winners and finalists are determined based on "overall excellence of presentation. The 8th Annual Beverly Hills Book Awards recognizes Front Porches to Front Lines by Simon Perlsweig in the category of Regional Non-Fiction: Northeast as a Winner.

National Indie Excellence Award

A leader and veteran of publishing award contests, The National Indie Excellence® Awards are open to recent English language books in print from independent, university, and self-publishers. Judging is now completed for the 13th year of this competition and the results commend a wide range of truly excellent titles. Front Porches to Front Lines by Simon Perlsweig is recognized in the category of Regional Non-Fiction: Northeast as a Finalist.

"There have been many books written about the impact of World War 1 and The Spanish Flu but for all that has been written, it is refreshing to read about the lesser-known and often obscure aspects of life, as opposed to the abstract national impact we are more familiar with. Intriguing or harrowing depending on the page Perlsweig writes in unsparing detail to make us feel fully present in his narrative. From descriptions of Springfield to his revealing and enthralling thoughts on Lawrence Reed and Gladys (Steere) Reed, few historians write with such fluency. And unlike many historians who are sketchy in the way they deal with the world beyond their principal characters, Perlsweig adds a compelling element of social texture to ensure his characters are vividly and emotionally depicted… It's through their letters that Perlsweig conveys their bravery, their sacrifices and the memories they have no choice but to live with. Each of them is a testament to the bravery of those who ensure our continued freedom and way of life and those who enabled them. **The objective of any writer should be to hold the reader's attention. To want the reader to turn the page and keep on turning until the end and this is what Perlsweig does. A must-read for fans of 20th Century Social & Cultural History of the U.S. Front Porches to Front Lines is unreservedly recommended."** *(BookViral)*

"The author's brief account can be cacophonously diverse; one learns, for example, of Thanksgiving meals enjoyed by American soldiers in France, the nature of modern courtship, and homemade antidotes for the flu as well as the personal details of the romantic arc of Lawrence and Gladys' relationship. However, out of this patchwork of information emerges a rich tableau of American life during the period—one of great fear and uncertainty but also one of sacrifice in many aspects of day-to-day life. And although the author's account focuses on positivity, he acknowledges darker aspects of the era… Perlsweig's prose is unfailingly lucid, and the story of his relatives adds a personal dimension to this impressively researched study. An often captivating and edifying history." ***(Kirkus)***

"Such an impressive accomplishment." — ***Shayna R. Gopin***

"He is the first graduate of HHNE to have a book written, published and cataloged in his high school's library." — ***Daniel R. Page, HHNE***

"Having worked so long and hard on this book, it is wonderful to see the fruits on his labor and share in his achievements, even from afar."   *– Dr. Esther King, Psy.D.*

"To expand on World War One history was insightful and wise and his book will enlighten in a personal way."   *– Carmen Witt*

"What an accomplishment" *– Hugh Putnam, Springfield Art and Historical Society*

"Having finished his book, I applaud him for the time he took and the effort he expended in the process. It introduces the reader to an interface between the personal lives of a small group of people while setting them on a world stage. It's quite the experience."   *– Richard O. Benton*

"Coming as it does at the centenary of the close of World War One, his book paints a nice portrait of many aspects of the war's influence on young lives." *– Robert T. Gerrett*

"I am very impressed with his writing skill. The book is very interesting and informative about the history of the time. What makes it special is its connection to family history and his acute attention to details. It provides a unique picture if what was happening during that time period. He is very careful to be as accurate as possible with his presentation and still manage to keep it entertaining. The book could be a useful tool for students around the world. It's an impressive accomplishment."   *– Steven Perlsweig*

"I can't wait to get started reading his book."   *– Karen Blakelock*

Reed and Steere Families, Circa 1920

Front Porches to Front Lines

One Small Town's Mobilization of Men, Women, Manufacturing and Money during World War One

Simon I. Perlsweig

Foreword by Dr. Yael Schacher, Ph.D.
Introduction by Dr. Walter Woodward, Ph.D.

Scriptor House LLC
2810 N Church St Wilmington, Delaware, 19802
www.scriptorhouse.com
Phone: +1302-205-2043

Paperback ISBN: 979-8-88692-126-7
eBook ISBN: 979-8-88692-127-4
Hardback ISBN: 979-8-88692-128-1

"Break the News to Mother"
By Charles K. Harris
Published in 1897, Re-issued in 1917

Shop Floor – Bryant Chucking Grinder, Springfield, VT, 1917
Lawrence Reed is the man the furthest to the left

Dedication

"Behind them stood the entire American people, whose ardent patriotism and sympathy inspired our troops with a deep sense of obligation, of loyalty and if devotion to the country's cause never equaled in our history. Finally the memory of the unflinching fortitude and heroism of the soldiers of the line fills me with greatest admiration. To them I again pay the supreme tribute. Their devotion, their valor and their sacrifices will live forever in the hearts of the grateful countrymen."

General John J. Pershing

To the thousands of men and women who faithfully served the Allied countries, above and beyond the call of duty, both at home and abroad, during the First World War.

To the soldiers and nurses who dutifully served in the trenches and the camps and whose efforts paved the way for the United States and Allied nations to achieve a swift and decisive victory.

To the civilians, who despite countless personal, social and economic sacrifices; willingly and loyally supported the thousands of family and friends who were defending their nations overseas.

To the farmers and machinists, whose thousands of hours growing food and producing military supplies, such as ammunition, helped the soldiers achieve victory by keeping them well armed, fed and ready for battle.

To the hundreds of civilian volunteers, who willingly devoted countless amounts of time, money and supplies through numerous Liberty Loan campaigns, blood drives and other supply initiatives, such as the rationing of flour and sugar.

The patriotism, camaraderie, self-sacrifice and devotion of these countless men and women are all deserving of our respect, gratitude and admiration. It's to them that this book is dedicated.

**"Registered War Garden Under
Protection of State Council of Defense"**

J.N. Dingo Barnes-Crosby Co., 1918

Table of Contents

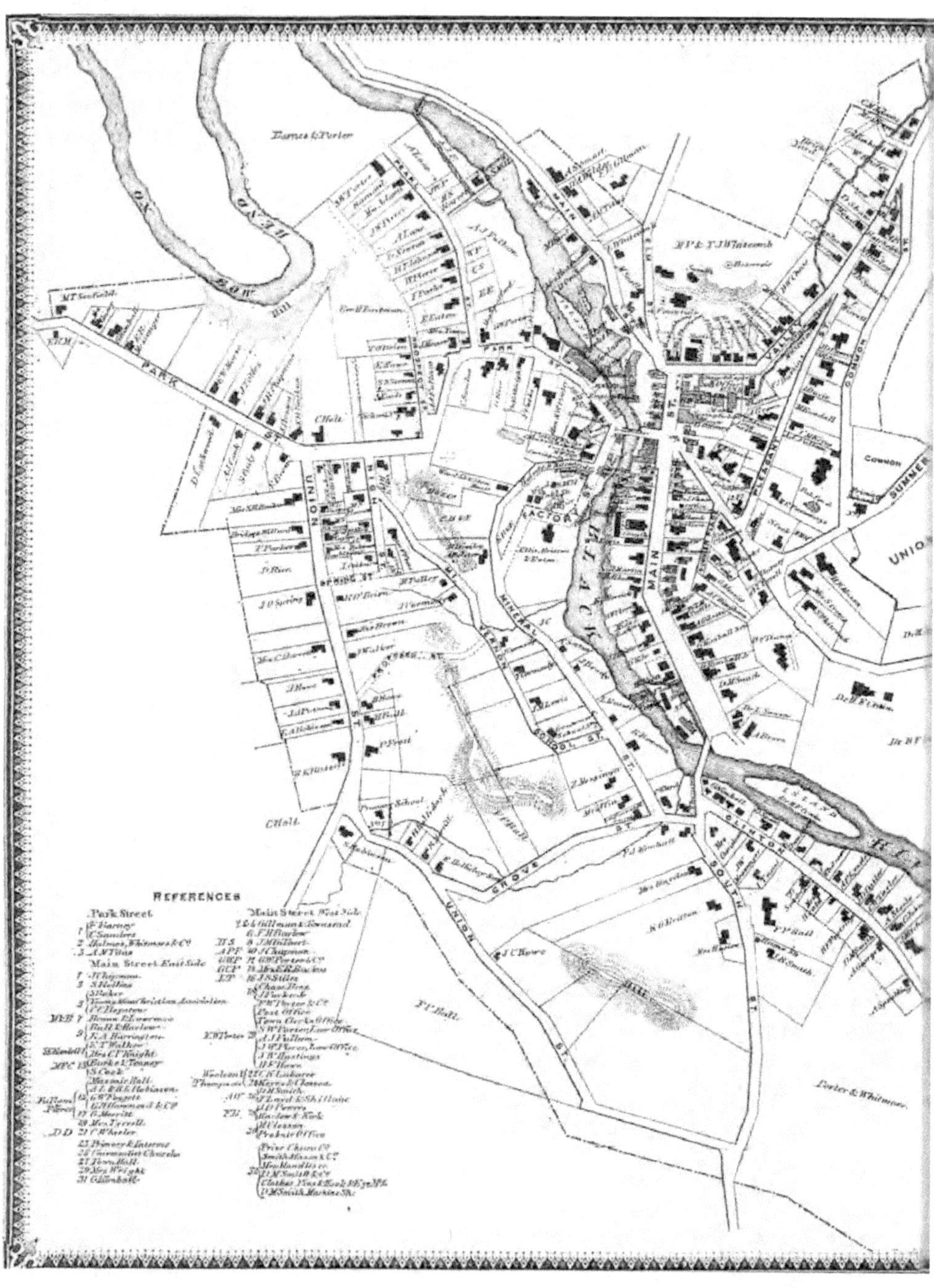
REFERENCES
Park Street
Main Street West Side
Main Street East Side

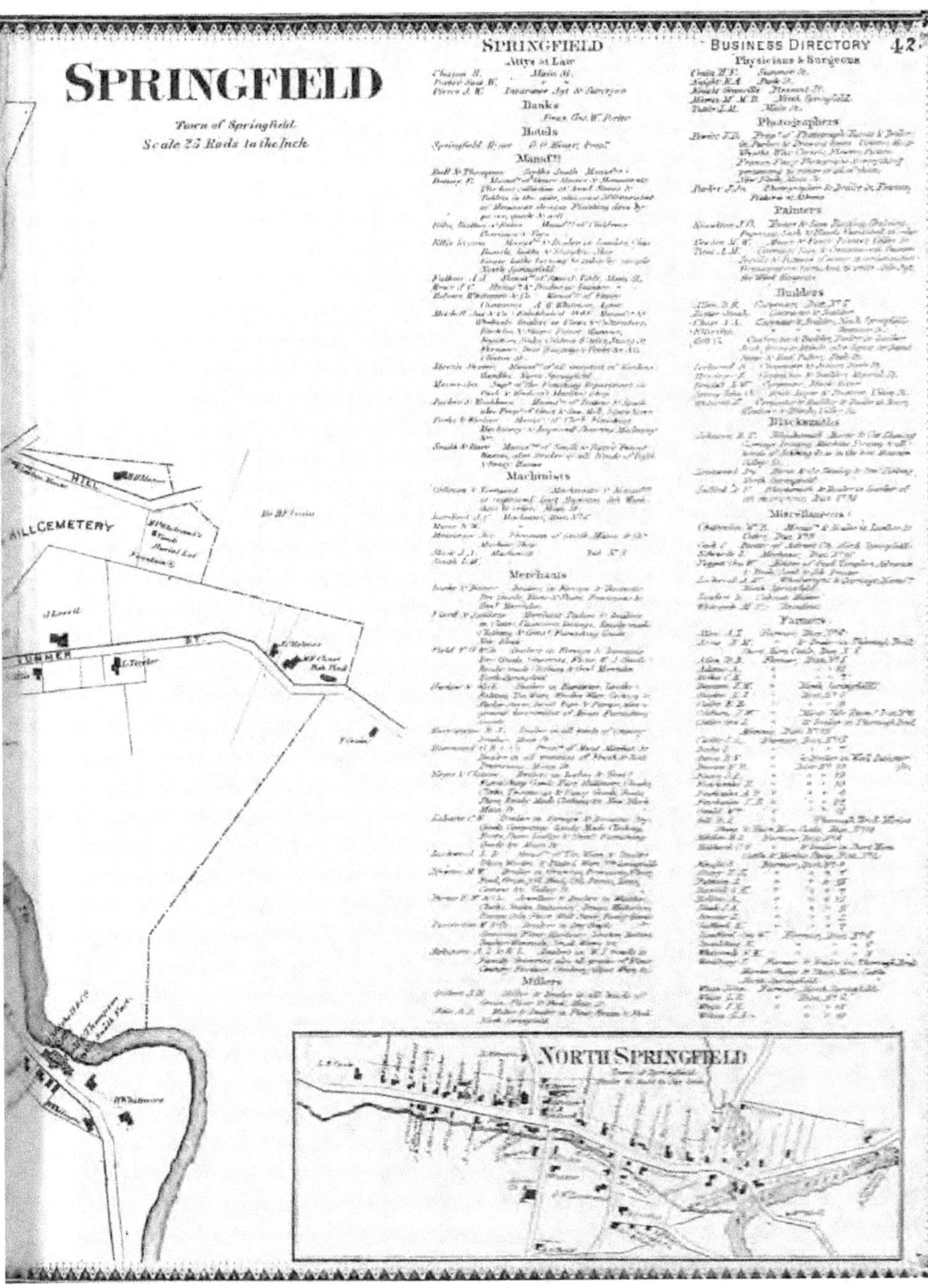

SPRINGFIELD
Town of Springfield.
Scale 25 Rods to the Inch

HILL CEMETERY

NORTH SPRINGFIELD
Town of Springfield.
Scale 25 Rods to the Inch

SPRINGFIELD BUSINESS DIRECTORY 42

Att'ys at Law
Banks
Hotels
Manuf'rs
Machinists
Merchants
Millers

Physicians & Surgeons
Photographers
Painters
Builders
Blacksmiths
Miscellaneous
Farmers

Armistice Day Rally – November 11, 1918
Springfield, Vermont

Foreword

In the fall of 2015, Simon asked if I would advise a project he had been working on about WWI-era Springfield, VT centered around the correspondence of his great grandparents. My interest was piqued as I had just completed my own historical essay with a letter at its center. In our first few meetings, Simon and I talked about methodology: how have historians most effectively used letters? Letters highlight the intersection of the personal and the political in history. During wartime, letters show how individuals think of themselves as historical actors on the homefront and the battlefront. This is evident in letters exchanged between Gladys (Steere) and Lawrence Reed. It was also put to use in Simon analyzes of chapters 4, 5, 6 and 11 of this book, which highlight the publicizing and circulation of private letters about the war in the Springfield newspaper.

What kind of story—about his family and about the war—did Simon want to tell using these letters? Simon had already written sections of this book that picked up on certain issues raised in the letters, but I wanted him to dig deeper into more of them. For example: How did the war change or reinforce workplace and factory policies? How did responses to the influenza epidemic highlight the community's divisions and priorities?

Simon sought out answers to these questions and explored many other issues (including the war's effects on courtship, the development of war gardens and flu remedies, for example). He also continued to contextualize events raised in the letters within a broader story. Simon and I had wonderful meetings to discuss sources; at a particularly memorable one, we compared the Thanksgiving dinner described in one of the family letters to 1918 Thanksgiving menus used by the army that Simon had found (see chapters 8 and 12). Readers, I hope I've whetted your appetites: this is a story full of historical detail and heart. Enjoy!

Yael Schacher, Ph.D.

Lawrence and Gladys Reed, Circa 1917

Preface

I never realized just how much of an impact one box from an attic would have on my academic career, when I re-enrolled at the University of Connecticut to wrap up a bachelor's degree in American Studies. Attics are the places where all those things no one has room to store in the main part of their home end up and sometimes these items can become completely forgotten. Anything from old clothes and toys to spare plates and silverware may be found in any of the dozens of boxes which inhabit one's attic.

A few summers ago, I was rummaging around my attic looking for some old files when I stumbled upon a box filled with letters. My curiosity coaxed me to go through this box and abandon my original task. I became even more enamored when I discovered that the majority of these letters were a correspondence between my maternal great-grandparents, Lawrence and Gladys Reed, along with a handful of other family members and friends. I immediately went to find my mother to tell her what I had found and to ask for a little clarification about exactly what I had discovered; aside from just a box of family letters. The box contained letters which were originally found years earlier in the homes of Lawrence Reed and Gladys's sister, Edna Steere when the family was cleaning them out. Some of the letters had been written during the First World War and my mother had always wondered if a letter detailing the Armistice Day celebrations in the town of Springfield, Vermont (where Lawrence and Gladys lived during the war) still existed. About an hour later, a letter dated November 17, 1918 and written by Gladys to Edna, surfaced and in fact turned out to be this "Armistice Day Letter." However, for the next couple years, that is about as much attention as this box of letters would receive.

Having a desire to do an internship as part of my remaining classwork at UConn, I remembered the box of letters and realized I could do a very comprehensive study of New England during the early 20th century based on the contents of these family letters. I very quickly drew up a proposal and presented it to State Historian and past professor, Walter Woodward, in the hopes he would be willing to be my academic advisor for the project. Being very intrigued, he agreed to oversee my proposal as an independent study project and I immediately began to gather additional resources, as I had already been reading and taking notes on the letters for a few months at that time.

While working on this project, the experience of doing mostly primary source research, both with the letters and in Springfield, Vermont at the local historical society, has taught me countless things about the research process. Most importantly, it has shown me how research has the tendency to expand via the "snowball effect." This means that every fact, quote or idea one gathers during the research process has the potential to lead to ten new facts, quotes or ideas, each of which can lead to ten more and so on and so forth. This research process has the potential to grow and develop a story exponentially! The more research I conducted, the broader the scope of the story became. In this case a simple box of letters gave an insight into some personal family history (Reed/Steere) which led to the history of a town (Springfield) and finally the history of a region (Precision Valley). Not only has the process of writing this book taught me so much about both the topic and the research process, but it has also helped expand mine and my family's knowledge of our parents, grandparents and great-grandparents' early years. This book will focus on the impacts of World War One on Springfield, both from the homefront and battlefront perspectives. The homefront perspective will be described and documented through the text of letters written between my maternal great-grandparents, Lawrence and Gladys (Steere) Reed, and a few close relatives and friends; while the battlefront perspective will be seen through the observations and stories in letters written by local Springfield men who went overseas at the time to defend the freedoms and liberties Americans had come to cherish. These soldiers' letters, in some cases were published in each issue of the Springfield Reporter, the weekly local newspaper, when provided to the paper by the families and friends to whom the letters were sent. Having done a great deal of research on this topic, I think it is clear the First World War had a profound impact on every American; man, woman or child.

This book will examine just one sliver of the whole story, by discussing how the war impacted the people of Springfield socially, economically and politically. I hope this book is able to paint a picture of 1910s New England during World War One and the Influenza Epidemic of 1918.

Simon Perlsweig

Machine Shop – Armistice Day

Acknowledgments

There are many people whom I need to thank and for without whom this project would never have grown to be what it has become. First, I would like to thank my family whose contributions and support have been so important through this entire process.

I would first like to recognize my maternal great-grandparents, Lawrence and Gladys (Steere) Reed, whose courting letters and other correspondence provide the foundation upon which my book is based. The other person whose correspondence makes up this aforementioned foundation is, Gladys's sister, Edna Steere. Even though I did not have the privilege of meeting any of them, the process of reading and analyzing their letters has given me just a taste of the people they were and how they were perceived by their friends and family.

Most importantly, I would like to recognize Lawrence and Gladys's granddaughter and my mother, Abbie (Sikes) Perlsweig whose family insights, stories, memories and willingness to read and edit each draft has allowed for the creation of a thorough and accurate story. I also want to acknowledge those family members who have asked not to be mentioned, but whose contributions, such as half of my great-grandparents' correspondence, played key roles in this book's successful completion.

One nice thing about writing this book was the way it became a family project in more ways than one. Along with my mother and aunt, I would to extend thanks to my brother, Ben, who came up with numerous bits of source material during my research trips to Vermont. I would like to extend special thanks to two professors from the University of Connecticut, Dr. Walter

Woodward, Ph.D., for writing this book's introduction and Dr. Yael Schacher, Ph.D. for writing this book's foreword. Both Drs. Schacher and Woodward also deserve special thanks for being so willing to oversee the academic aspects of this project, including being patient enough to go through all their comments and revisions one by one during our meetings.

I also want to thank Richard LaPorta and Husky Trail Press for taking an interest and desire to publish my book. My appreciation for their willingness to work tirelessly and patiently with me throughout the entire publication process is beyond words.

I want to give thanks to the Springfield (Vermont) Arts and Historical Society, for taking the time to make the majority of their resources available to me in order to conduct some of my research. Their willingness to do this during a time of transition, which at times rendered some resources unavailable, cannot be understated.

Lastly, I would like to thank my friends and everyone from the local community who has taken an interest in my project, including the Connecticut Authors and Publishers Association (CAPA) and its members. By having support from so many corners, along with that of my family, this book has provided me a clear reminder and understanding of why historians do what they do to document the past.

Introduction

Ralph Waldo Emerson thought that all history is biography, and in a sense autobiography. We understand best and only, that history to which we can feel a direct personal connection. It is this perspective on history that has led to the telling of this story, the writing of this book.

Several years ago, a bright young undergraduate student at the University of Connecticut asked me to supervise an independent study analyzing a series of letters written between his great-grandfather and great-grandmother in the period surrounding the United States' engagement in World War I. Given that he was a good student and we were approaching the centennial of the Great War, I readily agreed. I made clear to him however, that at the end of the day this could not just be a family story, though a family connection was the foundation for his interest. To succeed as a history project, I insisted, Simon Perlsweig's study would need to illuminate the greater issues connected to the war that shaped his great-grandparent's lives.

At the end of the project, I was impressed. Simon had taken a collection of family letters written to and from a small manufacturing town in Vermont, illuminated them with an impressive amount of background research, and put together a very interesting narrative of a World War I courtship in northern New England. He had not only written a compelling story, he had unpacked a series of questions about how a particular locale responded to a global war that cried out for further research. This, I told him as I gave him the "A" he had earned, has the potential to become a really useful and engaging book. I don't say such things very often – only once or twice in my career have I said this to an undergraduate student – and to tell the truth, I never actually expected such a book to really materialize. People lead busy lives, life takes them in different directions, and dreams deferred dissipate.

So imagine my surprise a few months ago when Simon and I reconnected at a talk, and he announced that his book would soon be published. Simon had not only taken the idea of publishing his study and run with it, he had slogged through the trenches of doing hard and careful research to make it a book of substance, one many people – not just family members – would want to read, and surely learn from.

Front Porches to Front Lines: One Small Town's Mobilization of Men, Women, Manufacturing and Money during World War I is a well-told, well-researched, and nicely imaged story of how World War I came to and changed the lives of a family (the Reeds), a town (Springfield, Vermont) and a region (the Precision Valley). It is a tale of courtship and family, love and war, disease and struggle, and the human capacity to adjust, survive and prosper. It is also a labor of love, by a most capable student who cared enough to make the possible real. This is his family's story. It is his story. It is our story, too.

Walter W. Woodward, Ph.D.
State Historian of Connecticut

BRYANT

Yes—the Bryant method of hole grinding is unusual—

but that feature fades into insignificance when compared with the remarkable hole grinding production which this design makes possible.

The machine tool world is now quite familiar with the radical design of the Bryant Grinder. The swinging wheel head, suspended from the overhead slide bar, presents many obvious advantages—markedly revealing an ease of accuracy on a ratio of 2 to 1, and a decided ability to push the wheel into the work without loss of rigidity.

But on the basis of Production—that vital test of any machine—we want to discuss with you the Bryant possibilities on your work. Let us estimate Bryant production time on your hole grinding; and write for the Production Book, which contains examples of hole grinding of almost every kind.

BRYANT CHUCKING GRINDER COMPANY
SPRINGFIELD - - - - - VERMONT

The Chucking Grinder

Front Porches
to
Front Lines

Chapter 1
Prelude to War

In the early 20ᵗʰ century, the northern New England States were primarily made up of small towns and villages, much like they were one hundred years before when the United States was still a very young nation with the majority of its states having at least a few miles of Atlantic coastline. Despite having experienced the Industrial Revolution in the mid to late 1800s, only a handful of places had developed into larger cities in order to accommodate the large number of new jobs created by all the growing manufacturing capacity. One of these places which benefited from the growth in manufacturing was Springfield, Vermont, a town which grew by nearly two-thirds from 2,881 people in 1890 to 4,784 people in 1910. This large population growth can be attributed to the number of machining jobs which came from the four machining companies which set up shop in Springfield between 1888 and 1916, including the Bryant Chucking Grinder Company, founded in 1909.

The first question, one might ask, is why any machining company would want to set up shop in a small town like Springfield, Vermont especially considering the town's relatively small population. The answer has three parts.

The first attribute which made Springfield a desirable location for machining companies is the Black River. The primary source of power used by large manufacturing plants in the late 19ᵗʰ and early 20ᵗʰ centuries was water power. Being situated on the Black River made Springfield an excellent location for large manufacturing operations. The reason why the flow of Black River had enough volume and head behind it to run the power turbines in several machining companies was because of the several waterfalls along the river's path; which drops about 100 feet over a one mile stretch through Springfield. Each fall gave the water flow more power to run multiple manufacturing operations. The hilly nature of the town and the waterfalls on the Black River were the product of the area being formed into a moraine by the retreating glaciers during the last ice age.[1] A moraine is a deposit of silt, rock fragments and other materials which a glacier pushes in front of it as it melts and retreats. The land mass which gets formed by these glacial deposits is typically a very steep, rocky formation with many hills and in a river's case, waterfalls.

Secondly, in 1887, Mr. Adna Brown, a Springfield businessman, approached the owners of the Jones & Lamson Company and promised to buy the majority of their stock if they would move their operation from Windsor, Vermont to Springfield. The owners of Jones and Lamson agreed to this if Brown could guarantee them ten years of tax-exempt status once they were situated in Springfield. The townspeople approved the tax-exempt status by a vote of 534 – 1 on December 3, 1887 and by August 1888, Jones & Lamson had a fully functioning factory in Springfield.

The third and last reason for Springfield's attractiveness pertains more to the manufacturing and other machining companies which would come later, all of which were started by former Jones and Lamson employees, starting with Edwin Fellows and the Fellows Gear Shaper Company in 1896.

Over the next twenty years, two more machine companies were founded in Springfield – the Bryant Chucking Grinder Company in 1909 and the Lovejoy Tool Company in 1916. These companies were started by William Bryant and Fred Lovejoy respectively, both of whom held top positions at Jones & Lamson when they each left to start their own company based upon either a new technology or a previously untapped sector of the machine manufacturing market. Bryant started his company around the production of a machine known as a "Chucking Grinder", which was a grinding machine with three grinding wheels on it, one for a hole's inside diameter, its outside diameter and its face or outside surface. By having all three wheels on one machine, Bryant had created one machine which was far more efficient than having three separate machines to complete the same amount of work. With funding from James Hartness, President of Jones and Lamson, production of the Chucking Grinder began in 1910, following the completion of a 20,000 square-foot factory on the Black River, just down the road from Bryant's former employer, Jones and Lamson. As the 19th century rolled into the 20th century, each of the machining companies in Springfield prospered in their own right. Not only did these companies bring jobs to the people who were already living in Springfield, but they also attracted many people from outside the area to come, settle down and raise their families in Springfield; including one of this story's principle characters, Lawrence Reed, who came to Springfield in 1915 to work at Bryant Chucking Grinder as a machinist. By the time World War One broke out in Europe in 1914, three of these four companies had already been through at least one expansion of floor space and production capacity as well as seeing an overall increase in sales as the years went on, including dramatic increases once the war began. Each of the three newer companies was also granted the same ten-year tax-exempt status initially granted to Jones & Lamson.

August 4, 1914 – This was the day Germany sent their first troops into Belgium, thus reneging on their promise not to violate the nation's neutrality, while attempting to recapture the hotly contested region of Alsace-Lorraine from the French; which the Germans believed would provide them the shortest route to Paris, as the Kaiser looked to expand his empire further westward.[2] Alsace-Lorraine is a region on the French-German border which the two countries had been fighting over since in the mid-16th century. In light of Germany's actions, Great Britain moved quickly to defend her two allies, Belgium and France, by declaring war on Germany later that same day and thus triggering World War One. As a result, U.S. President Woodrow Wilson quickly took steps to declare what the United States' intentions were when it came to which side they were or were not going to take in the upcoming fighting.

On August 19th, Wilson went before Congress and made public, his policy of neutrality and his desire to keep the United States out of the war by every means possible. As such Wilson was leaving the United States' Western European Allies such as the British and the French at the mercy of the Germans. Wilson also did not want to get the U.S. involved in a global conflict by which it wasn't directly threatened. "The people of the United States are drawn from many nations, and chiefly the nations now at war… Such divisions amongst us would be fatal to our peace of mind… the one people holding itself ready to play a part of impartial mediation."[3] After all, up to that point, not only had the United States already fought five major wars in its short 138-year history, it had also seen a major influx of immigrants from all over Europe, who Wilson feared might turn on each other or other Americans if the United States took sides in the fighting. Any such action taken by these new immigrants would probably have been the result of some old allegiances the immigrants may have still had to their mother countries, which Wilson feared might incite undesired civil warfare between the different immigrant groups. In 1914, Wilson's policy of neutrality was so widely accepted, not only was he able calm the minds of the people, he was also able to win a second term as president in 1916 mostly on the slogan, "He kept us out of the war". However, this was all about to change, barely a month after the start of his second term.

On March 1, 1917, a recently intercepted and deciphered telegram appeared in newspapers all across the United States. Named after its sender, German Foreign Secretary, Arthur Zimmermann, the message laid out Germany's intentions to begin "unrestricted submarine warfare" on American ships as well as their desire to form an alliance with Mexico and Japan in the hopes of keeping American troops occupied with a battle on their own soil; which would render the United States unable to aid her allies in Western Europe. Within days of its publication, the United States put an immediate end to all diplomatic relations with Germany. The appearance of the telegram in American newspapers also set off the reaction Wilson and Walter Hines Page, the U.S. Ambassador to Great Britain had hoped for.[4] For many Americans, the potential alliance of Mexico, Germany and Japan represented nothing less than a nightmare, with some newspapers equating it to a German declaration of war.[5] Realizing many Americans viewed the Zimmermann Telegram as a direct threat to the United States, Wilson could no longer maintain his policy of neutrality. On April 2nd, he went before Congress to call for a declaration of war on the German Empire, a motion which was overwhelmingly passed four days later – 82 to 6 in the Senate and 373 to 50 in the House of Representatives.

With the United States' entry into World War One in 1917, Bryant Chucking Grinder, among other companies, would have a profound impact on the war effort both at home and abroad; from providing jobs for the people in Springfield who were on the homefront, to the defense contracts the company negotiated to produce artillery and bullet shells in support of the American troops who were overseas in France, Germany and England at this time.

Despite indications of a direct threat to United States soil, there were still a large number of Americans who found the idea of getting involved in World War One to be distasteful. Not much could better represent Americans' sentiments about the war in late 1916 and early 1917 than the re-election of President Wilson on his promise to keep the United States out of a war which was predominantly a struggle between the major European powers of the time. However, as soon as Congress authorized Wilson's Declaration of War on April 6, 1917, Americans quickly began looking for ways to contribute to their country's war effort. Almost immediately, men began enlisting in the army, while women began volunteering for the Red Cross.[6] One U.S. official, when assessing the response of the American people to this new threat to their security and freedoms, claimed, "never had America known such a whirl of patriotic energy and self-sacrifice"[7] and the people of Springfield were no exception – the women contributing by volunteering with various service organizations, while the men who didn't serve in the military, for the most part worked in one of the local machine shops, many of which had been awarded government defense contracts.

The two principal characters in this story are Lawrence Reed and Gladys (Steere) Reed, both of whom were born and grew up near Springfield,

Massachusetts. Lawrence grew up in the Springfield suburb of West Springfield; while Gladys spent her early years in the small town of Agawam, MA in a rural section known as Feeding Hills, approximately six miles to the west of Springfield. However, their families came to the Springfield area in very different ways. Lawrence's parents, Norman and Josephine (Marcotte) Reed, settled in West Springfield in the mid-1890s, shortly after getting married. They'd met on the Hoosac Tunnel project, where Norman was one of the workers and Josephine was a cook in the workers' camp. The Hoosac Tunnel, which runs through the Hoosac Range between the Massachusetts towns of Florida and North Adams, had been in use since the 1820s and was having its central shaft expanded[8] at the time Norman and Josephine met around 1890. Gladys's family on the other hand came to the Springfield area under much different circumstances and had been there much longer. Gladys's mother's family, the Kings, came to the region around 1756, having been given a land grant by Great Britain's King George III. Her family had lived on that same plot of land ever since. The family name remained King, until Gladys's grandparents' generation produced only daughters, one of which was Gladys's mother, Della King. The family name became Steere when Della married Gladys's father, Dexter Steere, whose family was an offshoot of the Steeres of Northwest Rhode Island. Even though their families both lived in the Springfield area, Lawrence and Gladys's paths probably never crossed until Gladys began to board with Margaret Brown in the fall of 1910 in order to attend West Springfield High School. Even though Lawrence was of high school age at this time, he never attended school beyond the age of 12 because his stepfather, George Berry, demanded he leave school at that time in order to begin working. Gladys had to go to West Springfield for high school because Agawam/Feeding Hills did not have their own high school at this time. Presumably Lawrence and Gladys first met at the Methodist church in West Springfield that fall where the Reeds, Lawrence's family, and Margaret Brown were both regular attendees. It was very important to both Gladys and her family that she board with someone who was a member of the local Methodist church, in order to maintain consistency in her religious upbringing. Lawrence and Gladys probably saw each on a regular basis, both in church and around town as well over the next several years until 1915, when Lawrence moved up to Springfield, VT to work at Bryant Chucking Grinder and Gladys began attending Westfield Normal School to complete a teacher's certificate.

Chapter 2
Courtship

By April 1915, Gladys had been working on her teacher's certificate for about eight months and Lawrence had been working at Bryant for approximately three months. This was the time when Lawrence and Gladys began to write letters to each other on a regular basis; starting with a postcard which Gladys sent to Lawrence sometime in the middle of April. For the next seven months, these two 20-year old young adults wrote letters to each other on a weekly basis, but just as two friends, each one checking in on the other and updating the other on how each of their lives were week by week. However, all of this was about to change when someone close to both of them made a rather astute observation and suggestion.

On November 28, 1915, Lawrence received a letter from Margaret Brown, Gladys's Landlady, in which she advised Lawrence, "Write her (Gladys) a good letter and she'll answer it with one equally good… I think you'd make a very good match. I'm not match making but only giving you some advice."[9] Having had the opportunity to see both of them in action for so long, together and separately, particularly during their teenage years as they molded themselves into young American adults, Margaret Brown probably had as good an understanding of Lawrence and Gladys, both individually and together, outside of their respective parents and families. Therefore, she felt comfortable with rendering her amateur opinion about how good a match she thought Lawrence and Gladys would be for each other. Whether or not she ever rendered this opinion to just Lawrence or to both him and Gladys is unknown. However, as time went along, it is clear, maybe this amateur opinion was more wise and prophetic than it originally may have seemed. Immediately, the tone and content of Lawrence and Gladys's correspondence dramatically changed from just letters between friends to letters filled with many more emotions and feelings as the two of them began an active courtship.

The process which leads up to a man and a woman getting married, known as a courtship, went through a couple transitional phases in late 19th and early 20th centuries, as did the social attitudes and philosophies which governed marriage itself. For centuries, marriage was an arranged institution which was agreed upon by a young man's parents and a young woman's parents. This agreement could be made at any time during prospective bride and groom's early lives, from just before birth to a couple of months before the wedding day. As a result, there were cases where the bride and groom in an arranged marriage did not meet each other for the first time, until the wedding day itself.[10] For many young Americans at the turn of the 20th century, the downside of an arranged marriage was they had no choice in who they married and as such were expected to grow to love or at least coexist with the person he or she was paired with, whether they actually cared for each other or not.

According to Beth Bailey, the social response to arranged marriages was the development of courtship, a process by which a man and a woman would take some time to get to know each other in order to make sure they knew, trusted and loved each other before actually tying the knot.[11] A traditional courtship around 1900 began when a young man would drop a "calling card" off at a young woman's home, typically on a Sunday afternoon because that was one of the few "free" times most people had. The reason why Sunday afternoons was one of the few pockets of free time a person had during a typical week was primarily due to their work schedule. Around 1900, many people worked either as farmers or in the factories. A farmer had to work seven days a week because some farm chores, like milking, had to be done every day, even Sunday and for the most part these tasks got completed during the first half each day, leaving their late afternoons and evenings a little more open. A typical factory worker in the early twentieth century would work 5½ to 6 days a week, meaning they usually worked on the five weekdays plus another half to whole day on Saturdays as well. This type of schedule left the entire day of Sunday open for the worker to engage in a variety of social activities, such as courtship activities.

A young man was considered a suitable match, if he had been formally introduced to the young woman on some previous occasion.[12] The young man would then be invited over to the young woman's home where the two of them would engage in some formal activity like playing the piano, singing in the parlor or making candy, while the young woman's parents supervised discreetly from behind a slightly, ajar door.[13] As the courtship progressed, the young woman's family would have the young man over for dinner and eventually, the potential couple would begin to engage in social activities, like taking a walk, without the young woman's parents needing to be with them to act as chaperones. Not long after the couple was given the freedom to do things together by themselves was the time when the young man would typically propose to the young woman, asking her to marry him. However, as the 20th century wore on, the courtship process for young Americans would continue to evolve and change.

By the time World War One broke out in Europe in 1914, the modern concept of "a date" was beginning to dominate the process by which young Americans got to know each other before getting married. Initially, a "date" was a slang word which was used in reference to prostitution and exchanging money for sex.[14] In the context of courtship, a "date" came to be known as an outing where a young man would take a young woman out somewhere to have a good time. Some of the places potential young couples were known to frequent when on a date included: movie theaters, dance halls and restaurants. This was the point in time at which the process of courtship began to shift from private venues like parlors to public locations, like those mentioned above. By 1910, dating had almost completely replaced calling as the predominant courting custom in the United States.[15] Dating was particularly popular among young Americans because it provided a level of companionship many of them had never known before, which gave them a sense of security by having someone to do things with.[16]

Marilyn Coleman credits World War One with permanently breaking many of the conventions of arranged marriages and traditional courtship. This was due to the fact that the demands of the war caused people to be sent to different places all over the world; whether as soldiers, as nurses or as factory workers such as machinists. As a result, a man and a woman who were courting at this time could potentially go from being separated by a few houses to being separated by the Atlantic Ocean and everywhere in between. However, there were many young couples who found a way to still maintain their courtship, despite a geographic separation, through letters and other correspondence. These letters also provided a strong base to support the development of the modern system of courting at this time, something which was further encouraged by both the Industrial Revolution, which gave people money to spend on dates; and the invention of the car, which gave young Americans a way to take their dates further from their parents' homes than ever before, making dates an even more private aspect of courtship.[17] The demands of the war also turned courtship into a process which was achieved almost solely through letters and other written correspondence, since the war very often sent the man, or sometimes both the man and the woman, in a courting couple to two distinctly different places in the country, if not the world.

In war, there are two kinds of battles, those in the field, which are fought by the soldiers; and those on the homefront, which the soldiers' families and friends back home tackled on a daily basis, with one of their top priorities being the ability to support themselves and their families, while their sons and/or significant others were on the front lines in France. One of the many battles fought on the homefront is the one which deals with how families and friends coped with the idea of being separated from their loved ones as a result of the war. The most obvious example of this were the young couples, either recently or not yet married, who the war separated primarily by sending the men overseas to be soldiers. However, there was also a group of young couples who became separated because the men had to take jobs in places far away from where their wives or girlfriends were located. This was the case with Lawrence Reed and Gladys Steere. During their courtship, these two young people were separated by more than just a couple blocks, with Lawrence taking a job as a machinist at Bryant Chucking Grinder in Springfield, Vermont – a job which he held before, during and after the war; while Gladys was working on her teacher's certificate at Westfield (MA) Normal School. Following the completion of her teacher's certificate, Gladys spent the school year of 1916-17, teaching elementary school in Middlefield, MA. From the very beginning of their correspondence, both Lawrence and Gladys made it very clear to one another, not only how much they each missed each other, but also how much each one looked forward to getting the other's letter every week. On different occasions, both Lawrence and Gladys made reference to how their correspondence helped, at least temporarily, relieve their loneliness each week. Lawrence in his letter of August 8, 1915 refers to Gladys's letters as being as necessary to him as the sunshine each day.[18] Gladys in turn echoes this sentiment by voicing how writing to him helps cure her loneliness. Gladys's feelings of loneliness came from being at school in Westfield, which was an area where she believed there were almost "no nice guys", particularly ones as nice as Lawrence.[19] The lack of men on the campus of Westfield Normal School could be attributed to the very few male students at the school along with the school's strict policies which almost completely prohibited male-female contact on school grounds.

In the early stages of their correspondence, Lawrence and Gladys used their letters as avenues with which to introduce themselves to each other, by talking about their daily lives with regards to work or school, their families and any significant bits of local news which they wanted to share. Lawrence also goes as far as calling Gladys's letters essential to his happiness (letter of August 16, 1915)[20] and as important to him as his paychecks.[21] If there was anything either of them may have feared might keep their courtship from progressing the way they both hoped it would, it was the fact the two of them did not live in the same town. Gladys in her letter of November 7, 1915 was still unsure about how successful a distance relationship could be.[22] If there was anything which squelched any doubts either of them had about the potential success of their distance relationship, it was Margaret Brown's observation in November 1915 with regards to how good a match she thought Lawrence and Gladys would be for each other.

Not only was World War One responsible for separating families and young couples, (not to mention the tremendous heartache and worry it caused everyone to feel during this tense time) job availability was another thing which caused these separations. Lawrence Reed and Gladys Steere became separated when Lawrence relocated to Springfield, Vermont in Precision Valley to take a job at Bryant Chucking Grinder, one of three machining companies in the region in 1915. When William Bryant founded his company in 1909, he did so having come up with his own design for a machine, the chucking grinder, while working as a top engineer at the Jones & Lamson Company. Before the United States entered the war in 1917, all of Bryant's facilities were focused on producing these chucking grinders, which were in turn sold for use at companies like Ford and Cadillac in order to produce parts for car engines. Bryant opened up his factory in Springfield because like his former employer, Jones & Lamson, Bryant was looking to capitalize on the great source of water power provided by the Black River to run his factory. This, along with the jobs created by the expansions of Jones & Lamson and Fellows Gear Shaper, as well as the founding of Lovejoy Tool in the coming years, are what attracted many men like Lawrence Reed from all over the nation to Springfield and the surrounding area. This area would come to be known as Precision Valley because of the many machine shops which were located in this area in the early 20th century, primarily along the Black River in Springfield.

As such, even though the war was still more than a year away as far as the involvement of the U.S. military was concerned, there were still factors at play which caused young couples to become separated by more than just a few miles; which in Lawrence's case was job availability. If Lawrence and Gladys wanted to see each other at this time, one or the other would have had to make the 95-mile journey on U.S. Route 5 between Springfield, VT and Springfield, MA to get to where the other lived. Given the distance and at first the lack of a car, getting together on a regular basis just for casual outings or "dates" was simply not practical for Lawrence and Gladys in the early stages of their courtship. Also, the strains and demands of Lawrence's job just did not permit him the free time to do that amount of traveling at any one time. When he first began working at Bryant, Lawrence typically worked an average of 50 hours per week, for which he made $15.[23] Also given his overwhelming work ethic and desire to work, he would very often volunteer for extra shifts, either when needed or to take the place of another worker who couldn't make it into work at a particular time. Lawrence was also known for coming into the shop voluntarily about one night a week, just to keep the night watchman company while he stood his post;[24] a post Lawrence would volunteer for himself on several occasions throughout his time at Bryant.[25] During these shifts, as or with the night watchman, Lawrence would make the most of his time in the shop by working at his machine and continuing to turn out product.

Despite these obstacles, Lawrence and Gladys still found a way to get together on the average of once a month; at times when he could get time off from work and she could find time in her busy school schedule. Even though they weren't able to see each other frequently, Lawrence and Gladys were able to maintain the progress of their long distance courtship through constant, almost incessant correspondence. By 1917 their courtship letters were beginning to be filled with more suggestive and provocative comments, such as, "Perhaps we can enjoy a night's rest in perfect happiness and contentment Sunday night… Nothing would please me better although I might be bashful at first."[26] Following Margaret Brown's suggestion that they might make a good couple, Lawrence and Gladys began their correspondence on April 30, 1915 with him writing her a letter on the aforementioned date. Lawrence would eventually memorialize this letter as the first one in their correspondence over thirty-one years after they were married in 1917 and nearly three years to the day after Gladys passed away in 1945. Lawrence put extra emphasis on the date by writing it in dark, bold print and then circling it. On the outside of the envelope, Lawrence wrote that this letter was the "1ST LETTER TO AN ANGEL 12/30/48."[27] While written on the envelope over thirty-three years after the letter it contained was written, such a note was perhaps a way for Lawrence to remind himself of the time when he and Gladys first began to have feelings for each other, even though neither one was ready to formally express them at the time the letter was written in 1915. As winter turned to spring in 1917, Lawrence and Gladys were happily making plans to get married at the end of the forthcoming June. However they, along with many other young American couples at this time, would soon be forced to adjust their plans, as a result of their nation's entry into World War One that April.

Chapter 3
United States Declares War

The United States' entry into World War One caused many young American couples to begin to wonder if they would ever have a chance to spend married life together before the war separated them; both physically and geographically. On April 8th, just two days after Congress authorized Wilson's declaration of war, Lawrence wrote to Gladys, "Now that war is declared with Germany I suppose it will keep you worrying about how soon I shall have to take my rifle and knapsack and march off to war to belong to the United States. Let's hope I shan't have to go."[28] While understanding his patriotic duty to his country, Lawrence at least attempted in this letter to ease Gladys's mind about the potential prospects of having to go to war by making his hopes about not going to war well known to her. At the same, despite these efforts, Gladys, like many other wives, fiancés and girlfriends at this time, couldn't help but worry about the man in her life and the potential danger he would face if he was called on to defend their nation overseas – a feeling which she willingly admits is more selfish than patriotic. Nor did Gladys share Lawrence's initial hope about not having to go to war – a sentiment which she expressed to him in her letter of April 10, 1917. "I try awfully hard not to think about it at all, but I can't help it no matter how hard I try not to."[29] Similar fears were also on the minds of many mothers, who began to wonder if they would ever see their sons again, after seeing them off before they were deployed overseas. However, if there is one thing a devastating event such as a war can cause, it's the ability to make a person grow up and mature a little faster than he or she normally would. By the time Gladys finished writing her letter to Lawrence, her attitude towards the war began to reflect the outlook Lawrence expressed in his letter of April 8th. "But I am going to be real optimistic and think that the war will end before you have to go."[30] Over the course of writing a single letter on a Sunday afternoon, Gladys appears to come to grips with reality when it came to how she would cope if and when Lawrence got drafted. She seemed to gain the understanding that in a war, not everything was in her control, but it was her job to support Lawrence, whether he spent the war as a machinist in Vermont or as a soldier in France.

Even though, many young men rushed to enlist in the army in April 1917 following the declaration of war, not enough were doing so to grow the army to the desired size of 10 million men in a timely manner. In order to quickly amass such a large army, Congress began to entertain the idea of conscription, otherwise known as a military draft, as a means of quickly raising an army large enough to be a formidable force in Europe.[31] As a result, many young men like Lawrence began to realize just how likely the possibility of heading overseas to defend their country was becoming. "I don't see how we young men can escape the 'draft of war' which surely will be passed by Congress soon. I am just the right age and other things that go to make me too adaptable to the army's requirements."[32] Being of the appropriate age (22), and most likely unaware of all the requirements the army had for acceptable draftees, Lawrence was probably scared of having to go to war, once the United States entered the fight. Also, despite expressing a hope for a short war which wouldn't involve him militarily a few days earlier, Lawrence's hope for such a war was very short-lived. He spent the majority of his letter of April 12th to Gladys talking about how with Congress beginning to entertain the idea of instituting a military draft, it seemed almost inevitable that he, along with many other young American men, would at some point be called on to defend their country and its freedoms on the battlefields of Europe.

Lawrence also understood just how sensitive an issue, the war was for all of the young women who would soon have to say good bye to their loved ones, not knowing if they would ever see them again. "I don't like to mention the possibility of my having to go to war for it only makes life more miserable for you… [and] I'll never go till I am driven there by the force of the draft unless you make me go before."[33] While he was not afraid of becoming a soldier, Lawrence assured Gladys of his commitment to her and their life together, by letting her know about where his priorities were. By saying he wouldn't commit to military service until he either got drafted or at her suggestion, Lawrence assured her their life together was his top priority. At the same time, he also took great care in saying as little he could about the war in order to keep Gladys's mind at ease, even if the army called upon him then or at some future date. "I hardly think that you will ever have to enlist by my making you and I don't believe this country will resort to drafting… I guess everything will be quiet and peaceable before long."[34] Even though Lawrence took great care to not talk about the war for fear of upsetting his future wife, it is clear Gladys's feelings and opinions regarding the war went through an evolving transfomation over the ten days after war was declared. In her letter of April 15th, she adamantly assures Lawrence she would never force him to enlist, but at the same time she continues to see a positive light in these troubled times by holding strong to two beliefs. One being that the United States would never resort to conscription to build their army, and two; the continued hope the war would be a short one.

Aware that Congress was actively debating the issue of conscription and wanting to spend at least a few days of married life together before Lawrence was potentially drafted, he and Gladys had a decision to make. Lawrence and Gladys had planned to be married on June 25, 1917, however, there was a rumor going around that married men with dependent wives and/or families on draft day were far less likely to be drafted than were single men – a sentiment which Lawrence brought to Gladys's attention in his letter to her on April 29, 1917. "I am told by a friend that I would not be so apt to be drafted if I was married."[35] With that in mind, Lawrence and Gladys decided to move their wedding date to the first Sunday in May when it didn't rain, which turned out to be May 20, 1917 – a mere two days after the Selective Service Act was signed into law.

Along with shifting the date of their wedding, the war also caused Lawrence and Gladys to change their plans for their honeymoon, particularly with regards to where they went. Initially, Lawrence and Gladys had planned to go to Washington, D.C. to see the many sights and monuments it had to offer. Lawrence also had a friend who worked in the area and was going to arrange to get aspecial letter for Lawrence and Gladys giving them special access to the restricted areas of the White House which the general public normally was never allowed to see.[36] However, from the time the war broke out, "the Capital of the United States (had) been carefully guarded and consequently, the admission to the White House (was) prohibited now."[37] Essentially, President Wilson put Washington, D.C. under close guard to prevent any harm from coming to himself or any other person or landmark in the area. Instead, Lawrence and Gladys ended up going to Niagara Falls and Buffalo, New York in late June for their honeymoon, during which they saw the play "Beware of Strangers", took a lot of pictures and did a lot of sightseeing including following the Erie Canal for a period of time.

From early April through the middle of May, the army had been getting recruits solely through volunteers known as enlistees. Needing to grow the armed forces to the desired strength of 10 million men faster than what the rate of enlistees was allowing, President Wilson signed into law, the Selective Service Act on May 18, 1917. The Selective Service Act required all American men between the ages of 21 and 30 to register for a military draft which would take place sometime in the late summer. Registration Day was set for June 5th and of the 9,586,508 Americans who registered that day, 619 came from Springfield.[38]

On June 5th, every man who registered for the draft was assigned a draft number which if selected meant he would shortly thereafter head overseas to defend his country, pending a draft physical. On July 20th, the first draft number, which turned out to be 258, was drawn at random from a bowl of sealed black celluloid capsules by a blindfolded Secretary of War, Newton D. Baker. Inside each black celluloid capsule was a piece of paper with a number from 1 to 10,500. Each of these numbers represented one of the 10,500 draft or "red ink" numbers. When a man's draft number was selected, he would anxiously await for the mail each day, looking for the letter which contained a special green card, telling him he had been chosen for active military duty and where to report for his pre-service physical. If he passed his physical, he would then be assigned to one of the many boot camps around the country for basic training, after which he would be sent overseas. By the end of the summer in 1917, sixty men from the town of Springfield had been selected for military service and reported to basic training, each after having passed his draft physical.

Even though Lawrence, whose draft number was 1867, was initially very fearful of having to go overseas, what he and his fellow machinists didn't realize was that none of them would ever have to go off to war. This was because as a machinist, Lawrence qualified for what was known as a "Class 3 Exemption". Under the provisions of the military draft, there were certain classes of individuals who were exempted from military service or ineligible for it altogether. If an individual was given a Class 3 Exemption, this meant he was exempt from military service because his job was deemed essential to the war effort[39] and since all the machine companies in Precision Valley had defense contracts at this time, their machinists, including Lawrence, were exempt from military service. However, the war also meant longer hours and less vacation time for men like Lawrence, who the shops needed to keep up with the large number of orders the military needed fulfilled so they would remain properly supplied with enough ammunition and artillery shells. Not only did Lawrence see an increase in his weekly hours, but also an increase in the number of nights each week he had duty as the night watchman at Bryant.

While the men of America made their impact on the war effort primarily as soldiers or as workers in one of the many factories which had defense contracts, American women also had their own ways of contributing to the war effort as well. One of the many ways Americans on the homefront, particularly women, like Gladys, contributed to the war effort was by having home gardens to grow some of their own fruits and vegetables. These gardens quickly came to be known as "war gardens" because they gave people a new source of fruits and vegetables aside from going to the store, which allowed American food distributors to send more of their produce to feed the soldiers who would soon be overseas as well as to aid the people of Great Britain and France who were dealing with food shortages as a result of the war. The concept of the "war garden" was laid out in the book, *The War Garden Victorious*, written by Charles Lathrop Pack, a wealthy American businessman and philanthropist, who made his money in the forestry industry. In March 1917, he organized the National War Garden Commission to promote his idea, which he saw as a way to increase the food supply in the United States without putting additional strains on the already existing agricultural land and labor.[40]

Pack was able to promote the concept of the "war garden" through pamphlets, books and town meetings, one of which took place in Springfield, Vermont on April 30, 1917. At this mass meeting, James Hartness, the superintendent at Jones & Lamson, promoted the idea and shortly thereafter "small plots of vacant land were allotted to people who wished to grow vegetables for their own consumption"[41]; including Lawrence and Gladys who throughout the war, maintained a small garden on a communal piece of land just up the street from where they lived.

Along with the war gardens, the people of Springfield, Vermont found a variety of other ways to contribute to the war effort. Many people needed a way to store and preserve the produce they were growing. To do this they took to canning their fruits and vegetables, something also widely encouraged by Pack and the National War Garden Commission. Canning also became a common topic of people's letters during war. In the letters between Gladys and her sister, Edna Steere, the two of them often compared how many cans of fruits and vegetables each of them canned in a given week. The types of produce which people canned at different times of the year included strawberries, raspberries, blackberries, tomatoes, apples, cucumbers, huckleberries, peaches and quinces. Aside from war gardens and its related activities like canning, the people of Springfield contributed to the war effort in several additional ways. These included buying Liberty Bonds, having "meatless" days; consuming "war bread, a brownish but not noticeably coarse bread"[42] and establishing a rationing system for products like sugar and coal – one of which was overseen by a local committee, while also relying each person and family to use only as much of each product as was allotted to them each month. All of these adaptations which people made to their daily lives allowed more money and food to be redistributed to the soldiers overseas. Springfield, like many towns across the country, also established a local branch of the American Red Cross which took place at a dinner on April 25, 1917.[43] By July, the Springfield branch of the American Red Cross had shipped "eight dozen surgical skirts, 24 sets of hospital pajamas, 100 yards of cotton for bandages and 100 hot water bottle covers"[44] overseas.

In the interest of the war effort, the people of Springfield, along with thousands of other Americans, also agreed to lower their consumption of products like sugar, flour and coal. This concerted effort to cut back on the consumption and use of these and other products was adopted so the army would have adequate stores of all the necessary food and supplies it needed to feed and support its soldiers. There were also several items which the government chose to increase the prices of via war taxes. These included coffee, tea and movie tickets (one of the main forms of entertainment in Springfield).

Along with the production of Red Cross supplies, the other area in which the people of Springfield went above and beyond what they were expected to contribute to the war effort was the purchasing of war bonds, also known as Liberty Loans. These war bonds came in denominations ranging from $50 to $100,000 and featured pictures of former U.S. presidents including George Washington, Thomas Jefferson and Abraham Lincoln among others. In the first three months of the war, the residents of Springfield purchased over $304,000 of Liberty Loans, which was more than two and a half times the amount the local treasury department expected the citizens of Springfield to buy during the entire year of 1917. The incredible response of the residents of Springfield, when it came to the total value of the Liberty Bonds they purchased, can be attributed not only to their patriotism, but also to the widespread economic success which many of these residents enjoyed due to the full scale production of the four major machining companies located in Springfield.

Even though machinists, like Lawrence Reed, were exempt from active military duty because of the necessity of their jobs to the war effort, some of these men had such a desire to be soldiers; they chose to quit their jobs in the machine shops and enlist in the armed forces anyway. As a result, the machine shops, like Jones & Lamson, had to look in other places to fill their now vacant skilled labor positions. By the end of 1917, Jones & Lamson had decided to fill these vacancies by hiring women workers, known as "war workers."[45] Jones & Lamson set themselves a goal of having a fully functioning separate department for their female machinists by June 1918, at which time they expected to have one hundred women workers fully trained and working. On the surface, it was a winning situation all the way around because the hiring of women workers made more men available to be soldiers. The new women's department would be kept separate from the men's on a different floor in the shop as well as have its own entrance, away from where the men usually entered. This was probably done to keep the men and women from intermingling in ways they shouldn't while on company time, while also making sure the presence of both genders did not hamper anyone's production on the shop floor. Even though the men and women who worked at Jones and Lamson occasionally took little jabs at each other through pieces published in the local newspaper, James Hartness's experiment of hiring women workers to replace the men who had gone overseas was ultimately very successful. This was because as long as the women workers were willing to pull their weight when it came to their daily production, they always had the respect of their male co-workers.[46]

Despite any fears they may have had about the war, the response of the American people to the threats to their country, their freedoms and their way of life, was better than any government official could have hoped. Men and women alike each found ways in which they could contribute to the war effort. When asked to describe the extent of the response of the American people to the war effort, an unidentified government official said, "Thousands of men accustomed to large affairs laid aside every former interest to place themselves solely at the disposal of the Government."[47] In other words, the men of the United States were more than willing to put their personal lives on hold to defend their country. The same official went on to say, "Everywhere, voluntarily, people bound themselves together for food conservation and the saving of supplies of every kind… Washington had only to suggest a wish, and the nation answered. Every woman aided the Red Cross, and every man contributed to the Y.M.C.A. or similar organizations."[48]

The job of the Y.M.C.A. and its members was to make sure the soldiers were cared for overseas by providing recreation and entertainment for the soldiers when they weren't on the front lines or in the trenches. What was absolutely astounding to the U.S. Government at this time was how little effort they had to make when it came to convincing Americans to do things to aid the war effort. Americans, without complaining, consistently came through when it came to doing what the Government asked of them in regards to the war effort. From the American Red Cross to the Y.M.C.A and the army, the surge in American voluntarism among both men and women reached high levels of sacrifice and generosity. The United States made it very clear to the rest of the world they were ready for whatever fight came their way, both at home and on the battlefield.

Chapter 4
Letters

Throughout the summer of 1917, life in Springfield rolled along with little interruption. Two major events which highlighted the summer in Springfield were the Rededication of the Methodist church in July and the installation of street lights in August. These, along with the regular topics of canning, who was drafted and other local events; made up the majority of the letters exchanged between Gladys and her sister Edna. In October, in an effort to boost the morale of the 600,000 American soldiers including approximately 50 from Springfield,[49] who were expected to be encamped overseas by Christmas time, the local branch of the Red Cross organized a collection to send a Christmas packet to each soldier from Springfield, to go along with whatever gifts they might receive from family and friends.[50] Each packet was going to include "writing paper and pad, some game, pencils, tobacco, cigarette paper or pipe, gum, vaseline, shaving stick (an early shaving cream), shaving brush, sweet chocolate, candy, ginger and new skin (liquid bandage)."[51] These "Christmas stockings" were to be shipped overseas on November 1st.

Along with the machinists, the other group of men whose jobs exempted them from active military service was the farmers. The men who worked in the machining and agricultural industries at this time were deemed essential to the war effort in order to ensure that the soldiers overseas had all the weapons and food they needed to succeed in battle. President Wilson assured these men that each of their contributions to the war effort was just as valuable as the contributions of each soldier. Wilson believed a true patriot was someone who understood the importance of the service he performed for his country, without questioning its monetary value, whether he was a soldier, a farmer, a machinist or someone else.[52] After all, a soldier who was unfed and unarmed couldn't perform his duty very well and it was the farmers and machinists who attended to each of those needs respectively.

There was no family in the United States for whom the war in some way did not raise the level of stress within it and one of the ways many American families coped with this stress was through writing letters to each other. In the early 20th century, letter writing was a very common practice in many American families, many of whom made it a weekly activity. Also, since telephones had yet to become a universal household item, letter writing was about the only way some people were able to keep in touch with each other, including Lawrence and his family. As Methodists, the Reeds and the Steeres, typically set aside Sunday afternoons or evenings for letter writing because it was one of the activities which the Methodist church deemed acceptable for their members to partake in on the Sabbath. However, due to his increased hours at the shop as a result of the demands of the war, Lawrence didn't always get the opportunity to write each week, which Leona, his half-sister, on behalf of his parents and siblings, took particular offense to. "You little wretch, have you forgotten how to write? Don't you forget that once in a dog's age we want to hear from you, young man."[53] Call it sisterly love, sibling needling or any other term which might refer to the good natured ribbing and teasing which takes place between siblings, it was something else which also intensified as a result of the stress of the war. For other families, it was their only way of keeping in touch with their loved ones who were on the battlefields of Europe.

Once overseas, many soldiers began to write home to their families, telling them about their experiences, what they saw and where they were situated. Later on, some soldiers' letters were also submitted to and published in local newspapers like the *Springfield Reporter*, by the soldiers' families, giving the local townspeople a more intimate taste of what a soldier went through on a day by day basis. Some families even sent Kodak cameras to their sons overseas to allow them to take pictures of their locations along with their letters. One of the first soldier letters to appear in the *Springfield Reporter* was published on November 22, 1917 and was written by Corporal Carl L. Lawrence on September 12th. What makes Corporal

Lawrence's letter different from some of the ones which would be published later on, is that Corporal Lawrence was not a soldier in the U.S. Army, but rather the Canadian Army. He was one of many Americans who desired to get into battle earlier than his country did, in order to defend his freedoms. Beginning in 1914, he and other Americans accomplished this by crossing the U.S.-Canadian border and enlisting in the Canadian Army. In his letter, Corporal Lawrence talks mostly about the life of the soldier off the battlefield and away from the fighting. "The canteens are located at places convenient to the troops and are designed to furnish the men with tobacco and quite a variety of things at a reasonable price. One can buy 10 cigarettes for 30 centimes (six cents) or a can of corn for a franc (2 cents)."[54] For the soldiers like Corporal Lawrence, the army clearly had a wide variety of products it made available to the soldiers in the hopes of giving them as many of the comforts of home as possible while they lived under the tough conditions of battle. At this time, Corporal Lawrence was recuperating from battle injuries suffered in France at a Voluntary Aid Detachment (V.A.D.) hospital in Turnbridge Falls, Kent, England. "Every week here, a lady, called an official visitor, comes around with a little book and asks if there is anything we want."[55] While the soldiers on the front lines had canteens to go to in order to purchase things like cigarettes, the army also made arrangements so the men who were recuperating in the hospital could have the same access to all these amenities. To do this, they sent a woman around the hospital each week to ask each soldier if there was anything he wanted and it was her job to make sure these soldiers were furnished with what they needed. Corporal Lawrence also made a plea to his fellow Americans back home to donate to their local Y.M.C.A. which was raising money to ensure the welfare and comfort of the soldiers. "Certainly read this letter to anyone who will listen, publish it from the house tops, cry it aloud in the land so that people will believe."[56] While Corporal Lawrence may not have realized his letter was getting published in the local newspaper; he appears to be someone who would have been in full support of the idea of making his and other soldiers' letters public, in order to give the people at home, a small taste of what life in the field was really like.

For the first several months the United States had troops in France, the letters written home by the soldiers talked about everything from the European scenery and weather to the daily life of the camps and towns in which they were stationed. There was also discussion about some of the more noteworthy policies the army implemented, not only for the soldiers, but the local European citizens as well. Sergeant Jack Hackett in his October 28, 1917 letter to his mother makes note of two particular policies – one having to do with a curfew and the other having to do with the treatment of German prisoners of war. In his camp, all soldiers were required to be in their barracks for the night by 8:30pm every evening and the prisoners of war in his camp were used to fix little problems around the camp, like repairing electric lights.[57] Another one of the policies the army strictly enforced had to do with what soldiers told their families and friends about where they were stationed at any given moment. In order to keep their regiment's location as secret as possible, no soldier was allowed to disclose in writing his exact location at any point for fear the Germans might intercept the letters en route and find out from them where the American troops were located; which could have helped them plan a more precise and successful attack. In order to prevent that from happening, the soldiers were only allowed to disclose their locations using phrases like "Somewhere in England" or "Somewhere in France". The material a soldier could include in letters and packages was governed by a set of regulations, outlined by General John "Black Jack" Pershing on June 28, 1917.[58]

In order to ensure the highest level of success in battle with the fewest casualties, the United States military took many precautions to make sure no classified information found its way into the wrong hands. For this, General Pershing implemented a system of field censorship, with regards to the items the troops could carry on their persons or include in their mail. Soldiers were forbidden to carry any documents which might be of value to the enemy, like military orders and maps.[59] When it came to letters, they could only be written in English and were not allowed to include photographs or any precise names of a soldier's location or division. Information like this could have been used by the Germans to plan and coordinate future attacks. There were very few physical items which a soldier could include in packages to home and most of them fell under the category of "spoils of war" like "enemy helmets, caps, badges, numerals and buttons."[60] Every piece of mail to and from the enlisted men was subject to censoring. Officers' mail was not censored because it was believed that they knew better than to include any contraband information or objects. When a letter or package got to the censoring office, it was checked by an officer for any illegal contents. If nothing illegal was found, the letter or package would be resealed and stamped "OPENED BY CENSOR."[61] If something prohibited was found, the censoring officer would attempt to remove or ink it out before resealing and stamping the letter or package. If the censor was unable to remove such content, the piece of mail would be confiscated and never reach its intended recipient.[62] The officers who did the censoring were chosen by the commanding officers of each company or regiment and each censor was sworn to never divulge the contents of the letters or packages because they were mostly of a very personal nature.[63] Similar sets of regulations were established for telegrams and telephone conversations as well.

Even though the soldiers were not allowed to talk about their locations by name, they were allowed to describe these places in their letters to friends and family back home. "It is old-fashioned, built in the old days. They all do their washing at the town pump in the square; keep the pig in the cellar and the chickens in the kitchen. About all that they seem to do is farming and everyone works, kids and all."[64] This is how Private Russell Gordon described the little French town outside of which his unit was camped. He provides a very intimate portrait of a French country town for his parents who in turn provided it to the readership of the *Springfield Reporter* by having the letter published in the December 6, 1917 edition of the paper. This is just another example of how the men on the front lines wanted to give just a little taste of the war to those back home.

As war rolled into its second year for the United States, the worldwide sentiment against Germany and Kaiser Wilhelm II continued to grow on a weekly basis. By the end of 1917, 18 countries, including Great Britain and France, had severed their diplomatic relations with Germany. Of those eighteen, eight countries, including the United States, also had declared war on Germany by the end of 1917. An additional two countries would declare war on Germany in 1918, while two others simply expressed disapproval of what Germany was doing, but chose not to take any formal action against the Kaiser's government. By the middle of 1918, the only remaining neutral country was Spain who also took no formal action against Germany due to the fact that while its government was pro-Germany, its populous was pro-Ally.[65]

The men from Springfield who were overseas constantly praised the virtues of their French hosts and hostesses in their letters back home. Lieutenant W. Henry Munsell always wrote glowingly about Monsieur and Madame Mannierre, the couple who hosted him and some of his fellow soldiers. The Mannierres gave Munsell and his comrades comfortable indoor quarters, while keeping them well fed and entertained. They also helped them with their French in order to make communicating with them and the other townspeople as smooth as possible. Munsell and his men in turn helped the Mannierres fix little mechanical problems around their home, some of which hadn't been tended to in over six years.[66] However, while the soldiers, like Lt. Munsell, were living it up a bit in what he called the "lap of luxury,"[67] the people back in Springfield, weren't quite as fortunate.

The Featured Characters

Lawrence & Gladys
Reed. c.1917

Edna Steere
(Gladys's sister),
c. 1915

Della Steere (Gladys's
mother), c. 1910

Leona Berry
(Lawrence's sister), c.
1915

Margaret Brown
(Matchmaker), c. 1912

Josephine Marcotte
(Lawrence's mother),
c. 1905

Evelyn Reed
(Lawrence & Gladys's
daughter)
c. 1919

This Certifies that
Lawrence A. I. Reed
of _Agawam Mass._
and
Gladys E. Steer
of _Agawam Mass._
were by me united in

Holy Matrimony
at _West Springfield_
According to the Ordinance of God
and the laws of _Massachusetts_
on the _20th_ day of _May_
in the year of Our Lord 19_17_
Geo. E. Sanderson

Mrs. Geo. E. Sanderson

This is to certify that
Lawrence A. I. Reed of
Springfield Ms and Gladys
E. Steer of Agawam Mass
Were joined in marriage
in West Springfield Mass.
by me this the twentieth
day of May 1917.
George. E. Sanderson
Clergyman

Lawrence and Gladys Reed's Marriage Certificate – May 20, 1917

March
1	s	David Eugene	Earle Nailor
2	d	Florence Rose Anna	Wilfred Dansereau
4	s	Norman Emerson	Fred L. Eastman
7	s	Rastislaw	Nikifor Baskevich
8	d	Sophia	Andrew Matusevich
10	s	Harvey Lander	George H. Bassey
11	d	Marguerite Genevieve	Clarence D. Thomas
13	d	Eva May	Ervin C. Balch
13	d	Albina	Antoni Smolnek
14	s	Oton Zacharyjarr	Constanti Bielski
14	s	Abraham	Kieve Chorney
16	s	Roland Ralph	Ralph H. Carlisle
18	s	Dimitri	Alik Bladyka
23	s	Heorhi	Andrew Krukosky
23	d	Evelyn Ruth	Lawrence A. Reed
25	s	Junius Olenth	Kenneth O. DeLarm
28	s	Louis	Harry LaFlame
30	d	Mildred Lena	Leon H. Barry
31	d	Joyce Amy	Arthur F. Bennett

April
2	s	George	Lucas Nimkovich
3	d	Anna Hartness	Ralph E. Flanders
8	d	Josephine	Joseph Ankuda
8	s	Adam	Adam Wilkiski
10	d	Florence Ellen	George Lambert

Birth Announcement for Evelyn Reed
(Lawrence and Gladys's daughter)
March 23, 1918

Gladys's Wedding Ring

Wedding Gifts – Lawrence and Gladys Reed, May 20, 1917

Gold Plated Thimble

Set of 1910s Glass Goblets

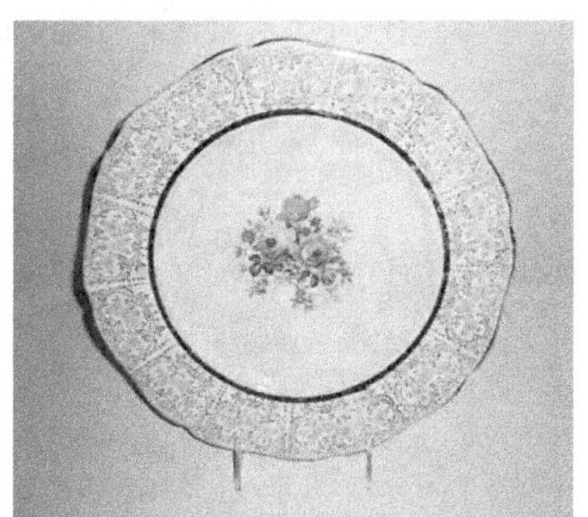

Cake Plates

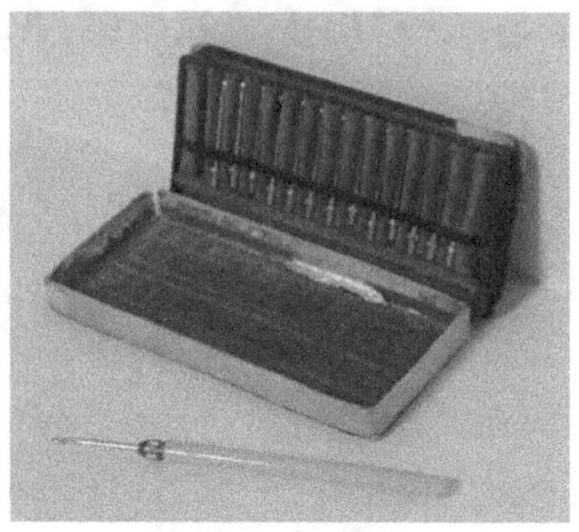

Set of Crochet Hooks

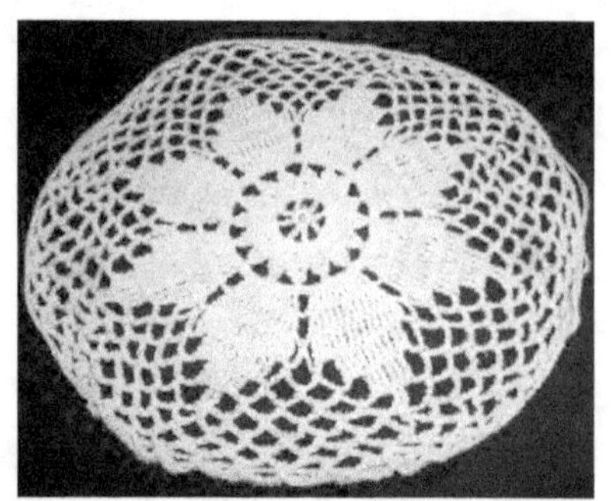

**Crocheted Doily
by Gladys Reed**

17 Furnace Street, Springfield, Vermont
Home of Lawrence and Gladys Reed
Still Standing, Picture Taken: June 2017

Trolleys used by the Springfield Electric Railway in 1910s, which connected Springfield to many of the surrounding cities and towns in the region. Currently Located at Connecticut Trolley Museum, East Windsor, CT

Sites Around Springfield, Vermont

METHODIST EPISCOPAL CHURCH—*Photo by Dressell.*
Dedicated in 1917

METHODIST EPISCOPAL CHURCH—*Photo by Dressell.*
Dedicated in 1842

The Ideal Theater – One of the few forms of entertainment in Springfield in the 1910s

The Arch Bridge & Black River Falls, 1915

The Black River Falls, 1915

The Arch Bridge & Black River Falls, 2015

Springfield Town Library

Town Square

World War One Era Sheet Music.
Owned by Gladys Reed who was an avid piano player,
especially for friends and family.

"Over Yonder Where the Lilies Grow"
By Geoffrey O'Hara
Published in 1918

"If I'm not at the Roll Call, Kiss Mother Goodbye for Me"
Written by George L. Boyden
Published in 1918

"Break the News to Mother"
By Charles K. Harris Published in 1897,
Re-issued in 1917

"Each Stitch is a Thought of You, Dear"
Words by Al Sweet, Music by Billy Baskette
Published in 1918

"Just a Baby's Prayer at Twilight (For Her Daddy over There)"
Words by Sam M. Lewis & Joe Young, Music by M.K. Jerome
Published in 1918

"I May Be Gone For a Long, Long Time"
Words by Lew Brown, Music by Albert von Tilzer Published in 1917

World War One Era Religious Postcards

Christmas

Easter

World War One Draft Card

Lawrence Reed's Draft Card
Draft Number: 1867

The 1st Registration took place on June 5, 1917 and was for men born between June 5, 1886 and June 5, 1896. Lawrence's Birthday: June 13, 1895.

Shop Floor – Bryant Chucking Grinder, Springfield, VT, 1917
Lawrence Reed is the man the furthest to the left

The Machine Shops in Springfield, Vermont

Bryant Chucking Grinder Company

Jones and Lamson Machine Company

Fellows Gear Shaper Company

The Women Workers of Jones and Lamson

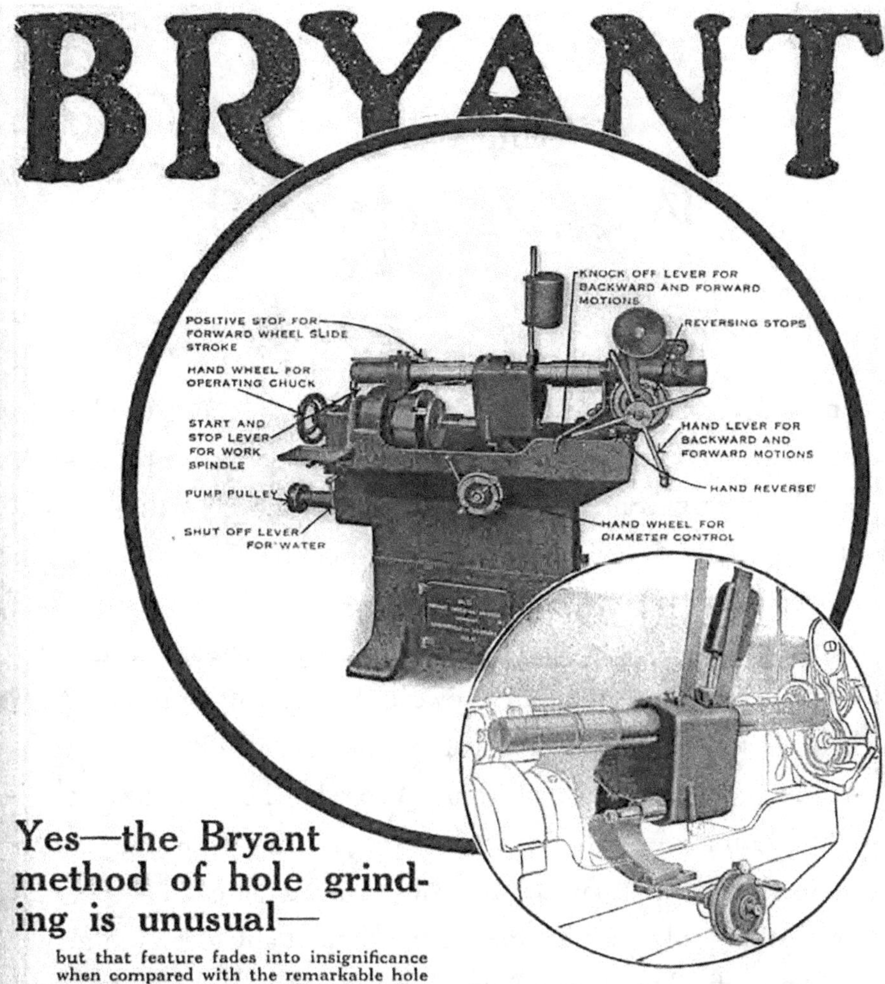

Yes—the Bryant method of hole grinding is unusual—

but that feature fades into insignificance when compared with the remarkable hole grinding production which this design makes possible.

The machine tool world is now quite familiar with the radical design of the Bryant Grinder. The swinging wheel head, suspended from the overhead slide bar, presents many obvious advantages—markedly revealing an ease of accuracy on a ratio of 2 to 1, and a decided ability to push the wheel into the work without loss of rigidity.

But on the basis of Production—that vital test of any machine—we want to discuss with you the Bryant possibilities on your work. Let us estimate Bryant production time on your hole grinding; and write for the Production Book, which contains examples of hole grinding of almost every kind.

BRYANT CHUCKING GRINDER COMPANY

SPRINGFIELD - - - - VERMONT

The Chucking Grinder

Chapter 5

Winter 1917-18

One might say that for the people of Springfield, no good deed or action went unpunished or came without a consequence or some fine print attached. The late fall and early winter of 1917 was a very tough time for Springfield's residents, especially the winter, which was exceptionally cold and snowy. Lawrence received his first leave from work since his wedding when he took off the Wednesday to Monday, which included Thanksgiving, to celebrate the holiday with Gladys and her family. However, to make up for those lost hours of work, Lawrence was required to work nights for the following two weeks straight through until 6am each morning. Also, while he was allowed to spend Christmas Eve at home with his wife that year, it meant he had to go into the shop and work on Christmas Day in order to make sure there was always someone working all the machines in the shop at any given moment. The people of Springfield were able to make it through such a tough winter by maintaining a calm and slightly humorous attitude about things, including one woman who, when her pipes burst, covering her pantry floor with ice, chose to hang a sign outside her home which said "Skating Rink."[68] While many Americans in places like Springfield survived the winter of 1917-1918, it was not always in comfort. The shortages of sugar, fuel and flour and the increased prices of products like coffee as well as the many instances of pipes bursting due to the severe cold didn't make their lives at this time any easier.

In some places the harsh winter along with the many other hardships which were a result of the war led to some unpleasant reactions from some people, often having devastating consequences for the communities at large. In Bethel, Vermont for instance, a woman became so upset due to a store's lack of sugar that she ran out of the store and returned a while later with a rolling pin which she used to smash the store's window.[69] The direct result of this bit of rash behavior was the imposition of a strict sugar-rationing system on all the people of Bethel.

Fortunately for Springfield, its people seemed to be of a much calmer demeanor and much more of the problem-solving   type as opposed to some of the people in the surrounding towns, like Bethel. Gladys in her letters to and from her friends, Carrie Merchant, a former schoolmate and Grafton, Vermont school teacher; and Margaret Brown, who was the "matchmaker" for Gladys and Lawrence, exchanged different ways and ideas for how to cope with the shortages they were facing, particularly with regards to flour and sugar. While it didn't replace sugar in all applications, Carrie found that using Karo worked just as well as sugar in most instances.[70] Also, by living in New England and as such being near the heart of maple country; Margaret found that maple syrup also served as a decent alternative to sugar in many applications as well.[71] "We use barley flour, rye, graham, oatmeal, cornmeal and every other wheat flour substitute."[72] Along with her suggestion of using maple syrup as a sugar substitute, Margaret also had several ideas for what to use in the place of wheat flour, most of which was going to the men overseas. Based on the short list given her letter of February 17, 1918 to Gladys, it's clear nothing was off the table when it came to searching for a suitable substitute for wheat. These stresses along with worrying about their loved ones overseas made life at this time very difficult for many Americans, especially when overseas correspondence was erratic at best. Gladys described most days at this time as being made up of the same three activities day after day – eating, sleeping and sewing;[73] much of the latter was done in the form of charity projects, primarily for the Red Cross, who were not only aiding the soldiers, but were also distributing handmade clothes to many orphaned children in France as well.[74]

By the beginning of 1918, the war was beginning to wear on the American public, especially those men who anxiously awaited the mail every day to see if that special green card came which told them that they had been chosen for active duty overseas and where to report to take their pre-service physical. Bill Gorley, in a letter to his good friend, Lawrence Reed, tells him, "Well I hope the war will soon be over as it is causing an awful lot of misfortune and hardships."[75] What Bill is referring to, is all the anxiety and worry the people at home experienced as a result of the impacts of the war. In Bill's case, he had the additional worry of the war costing him his job, because supposedly every employee at the Springfield (MA) Armory was required to buy a Liberty Bond in order to keep his job [However, since I was unable to verify this with Armory historian, Richard Colton; I have concluded that this requirement of every employee needing to purchase a Liberty Bond may have just been the act of an overzealous boss who was looking to make sure he filled his departmental quota of purchased Liberty Bonds. His strong language was probably a way of "encouraging" the men in his department like Bill to ensure the department quota was met].

Even though, many of their men were overseas, the people of Springfield, Vermont found several different ways to acknowledge and honor their service to their country and its people. On February 17, 1918, the members of the Sunday school class at the local Methodist church presented a flag with twenty-three stars on it to the church, in honor of the twenty-three men from the church who were serving overseas. The ceremony where this flag was presented was meant to demonstrate "those who have gone into the service are not wasting their lives; but rather, using them to put down wrong and exalt what is highest at best."[76]

With the arrival of March, came the arrival of spring and with it some renewed hope the war would be over some time in the very near future. "I think Germany will get a good surprise this summer. Let's hope so anyway."[77] Bill Gorley, in a letter to Lawrence, is showing some new optimism that the United States and the Allies will prevail over Germany in the coming months, putting an end to the Great War. Bill had an additional reason to at least be a little relieved. He failed his draft physical, meaning he would not have to serve overseas and could spend the duration of the war stateside.

In the first few months of 1918, the United States continued to amass their forces throughout France, while the attention of Germany began to shift towards the Eastern Front and the threat the Russians were posing as they charged westward towards Berlin. As a result, these first few months of 1918 were rather uneventful for many of the American troops overseas and as such gave them some additional time to absorb some French culture they might not have otherwise had the chance to appreciate, had they been fighting on the front lines. Sergeant A.C. MacDonald's letter of January 2, 1918, which was published in the *Springfield Reporter* on January 31, 1918 talked about what it was like to spend New Year's in France. "The French custom of wishing people a happy New Year is kissing them when you meet them… They (the soldiers) were kissing everything that looked good to them and did not seem to care what happened, as everyone was doing it."[78] Even though the French may have seemed a little cavalier to the stoic Vermont Yankees when it came to some of their celebratory practices; the soldiers, who were looking perhaps to live a little before having to go to battle, had no problem joining in the fun, no matter what the consequences might have been. As a member of the military police force in France, it was MacDonald's duty to maintain order and discipline within the towns and/or camps where he was stationed, which left him little spare time to engage in some of the native French customs,[79] like those of New Year's.

One of the ways the soldiers filled their time away from the battlefield was through competitive sports, during which two regiments camped near each other would organize teams to compete against each another. Two of the most common sports, in which regimental teams would compete, were baseball and football. Baseball impacted the war in two ways. Claude Barber, who was part of the 101st Supply Train of the American Expeditionary Force (AEF), in his letter of December 25, 1917, talked about how he and other men in his outfit celebrated Thanksgiving by playing some games of baseball and football before dinner. Unfortunately, some German artillery brought the baseball game to a premature end.[80] The other way baseball impacted the war, is represented by the many players who put their playing careers on hold to defend their nation.

One particular group, the U.S. Chemical Warfare Division, whose job it was to penetrate the German lines and destroy their chemical weapons; had five future baseball hall-of-famers in it throughout the course of the war – Ty Cobb, Christy Mathewson, Branch Rickey, Eppa Rixey and George Sisler. Of those five, Cobb, Mathewson and Rickey all served together in France. One of the reasons, so many great baseball men served together in the same unit was because the mutual respect and trust these men had for each other as baseball professionals drove their desires to not only serve their country, but to serve their country all as part of the same unit. As such, when players like Cobb and Mathewson went to enlist, they both requested to be assigned to the same unit as Rickey. By the war's end all three men had become officers in the specialized chemical warfare unit. Private Russell F. Whitney, in his letters, talked about how his squadron, the 53rd Aero Squadron, played several games of American football against teams from other local regiments and squadrons.[81] The soldiers constantly praised the way they were treated by the French townspeople, when it came to having comfortable quarters and being well fed, no matter where they were in France. This reassured their families and friends back home that they were always well situated, while being extraordinarily confident the war would be short-lived, a belief which the soldiers would have an opportunity to make a reality come the spring of 1918.

Even though the American soldiers played next to no active role in war during the late winter and early spring of 1918, the men spent most of their time getting situated in the French countryside where they would soon be fighting. American soldiers were mere spectators to most of the battle action at this time. Private Darwin Ransom in a letter to his mother talked about an air battle, he and a fellow soldier saw one day between French and German aircraft. "Following the German plane were two French planes, which were trying to use their machine guns on the Germans… The French plane looped the loop and came down on the German, this time using the machine gun on the enemy craft."[82] In this battle, Darwin and his friend witnessed the French planes shoot down a German plane which was later picked over for souvenirs by them and other American soldiers, as well as some French soldiers and locals.[83] Darwin ended up with a piece of the motor, a machine gun bullet cartridge and quite the story to tell, both to his comrades back in camp and his family back in Springfield. The soldiers were some of the best mouthpieces the different organizations, which were doing relief work overseas, had to promote their efforts and obtain support for their work. Private Russell Whitney, in many of letters home to family and friends, spent at least one or two paragraphs on the benefits and good work, organizations like the American Red Cross and the Y.M.C.A., were doing for both the soldiers and the local civilians.[84] The desire of the soldiers to actively support and promote the good work of organizations like the Y.M.C.A. appears to have been spontaneous. However, by April, the war was beginning to really wear on many Americans, who were tired of reading about a war in which American troops had yet to play a really active role. As such, it seems as though the American people were beginning to get fed up with the lack of activity being reported from overseas, while there also had to be some American soldiers who were beginning to wonder if and when they would participate in any real battle action.

Any combat witnessed by the soldiers, even if they weren't active participants in it, like the air fight to which Private Ransom was a spectator, was a noteworthy event and one worth writing home about. At the same time, the people of New England also made sure to take note of as many positive events as possible, even down to the arrival of spring as marked by the sighting of migrating flocks of robins and bluebirds back to New England, along with the sight of the grass just beginning to turn green. For the Reeds, March 1918 was a very memorable month because Lawrence and Gladys celebrated the birth of their first child, a girl (and my maternal grandmother) who they named Evelyn Ruth on March 23rd. For the next two weeks, Lawrence and Gladys were constantly receiving congratulations and well wishes from family and friends; while the trees and flowers began to leaf out and bloom all around them. Gladys really enjoyed taking care of the baby because it was something which she had never done before. It also gave her ample opportunities to exploit her creative talents using some of her time to knit things for her new daughter, including socks, sweaters and blankets while also receiving many similar items from her family and friends. Her mother, Della, told her having a girl was the right way to begin with regards to having children or offspring and how, her father, Dexter, now felt really old since he was now a grandfather. With very little American involvement in the war up to this point; the men overseas still found ways to fill their free time. Meanwhile, their families and friends back home spent their time celebrating major life events like births and weddings. Just as Lawrence and Gladys's lives became more interesting with the birth of Evelyn, the lives of the troops were also about to get a little more exciting as well.

Chapter 6
Cantigny and Points East

By the end of May, the garden which Lawrence and Gladys were helping to tend, just up the road from their house, was beginning to show signs of life as the first vegetable plants began to sprout; specifically asparagus, sweet peas and potatoes. They also began to find wild berries along the sides of the roads as well as several dozen types of flowers, which were currently blossoming. At this point in time, Gladys's favorite thing to write about was her young daughter and the ways Evelyn managed to impress, if not sometimes scare Gladys with her rapid growth and sense of adventure, even at only a few months old. Unfortunately for Lawrence though, he didn't always have the opportunity to see the development of his daughter because of the long hours he needed to work at the machine shop. He even had to miss some family trips to visit his in-laws because he was unable to obtain the leave time needed in order to go. On June 15, 1918, Lawrence and the other men at Bryant were told that no one would be allowed any vacation time that year due to the demands of the war. When he was home by himself and not working, Lawrence would spend hours working in and tending the garden. He also was called in to take a draft physical at the beginning of the month, but was exempted from service for two reasons – one, was because of the job he held at Bryant which was deemed essential to the war effort; and two, was a medical disqualification due to his flat feet.

In April 1918, one year after the United States declared war on Germany, the American forces engaged the enemy troops in battle for the first time. The first soldiers' letters to tell of some early battle action witnessed by United States troops and be printed in the *Springfield Reporter* were written by George B. Wilder to his mother in March and April and published on May 16, 1918. One of the main battle tactics used during World War One was trench warfare. In trench warfare, a tactic used by both the Allies and the Central Powers, the soldiers would dig a ditch in the ground and use it both as a battle position from which to shoot at the enemy troops as well as a fortification for protection from opposing gunfire. However, life in these six foot deep channels was no picnic for any soldier. The Allied soldiers were constantly under fire from enemy artillery and the facilities for personal hygiene were improvised and less than adequate.[85] "In the trenches it is customary to see men shaving – using anything for a mirror."[86] As a result of these poor conditions and in an effort to clean up a little, the first thing a soldier tended to ask for upon returning from his shift in the trenches was soap.[87] Life in the trenches also tended to be very dull for the troops, if they weren't actually engaged in any fighting. The soldiers passed the long spells of inactivity by playing games, talking amongst themselves and wondering if they would have the "privilege" of engaging the enemy in one of the rare bayonet charges. A bayonet charge was one of the few opportunities the soldiers in the trenches had to engage in hand-to-hand combat.[88] While the men didn't necessarily mind the incessant artillery barrage, they became rather disgusted when forced to skip a meal, particularly breakfast. Perhaps the best part of trench life was it gave the soldiers from several countries a chance to bond and build camaraderie while learning about each other's lives and cultures.

According to Wilder, a private stationed in France with the 103rd Infantry Division, when soldiers weren't engaged in battle, they didn't necessarily spend all their time in the trenches. During these times, the soldiers would do shifts in the trenches – four weeks in and then three weeks out. Also, in the spring of 1918 and in preparation for battle, the soldiers also began going on very long hikes as a unit(s). One particular hike, according to Wilder, covered fifty-two miles in four days. "For breakfast we have two or three slices of bacon, a spud, bread and coffee… At noon we are given roast beef, potatoes, onions, bread and coffee."[89] In the early months of 1918, letters written back home by Wilder and other soldiers tended to stick to a very select number of topics including the soldier's diet and daily routine, the area where he was encamped, the local townspeople and any other noteworthy events; like any air combat he witnessed. However, the soldiers' letters would begin to take on a new focus after the American forces engaged in their first offensive action of World War One at the Battle of Cantigny on May 28, 1918.

Cantigny was a small French agricultural village, with about 100 people and a few small businesses, which lay 72 miles north of Paris and 65 miles east of the English Channel.[90] While Cantigny changed hands several times during the war, it most recently had been captured by the Germans back on April 5, 1918.[91] The town itself was of little military value, except that since it was situated on a plateau, several hundred feet above the surrounding land, it gave the Germans a position of strength and a full view of the Allied troops who were gathering all around them. For many of the soldiers from Springfield, Cantigny must have brought back some memories of home, given its small town and agrarian nature. By May 28th, the Americans had amassed enough troop strength in the area to go on their first major offensive of the war. Starting at 4:45am, the American troops began shelling Cantigny and the Germans within it. Within three and a half hours, the American troops, with cover from French tanks, drove the Germans out of and recaptured Cantigny. However, it would take three days to secure the town and repulse the final German counterattack. While the battle was overall small in nature, it proved to all the European powers that the American Expeditionary Force was capable of fighting and winning a battle. Even though the victory at Cantigny was small compared to some later engagements, it was a major morale and confidence booster for the American soldiers themselves.[92] This was the first time the German advance across Western Europe had been stopped and it would be closely followed by two other Allied victories at Chateau-Thierry and Belleau Wood in the following weeks, as the Americans began to turn the tide of the war against the Germans.

Following the victory at Cantigny, the morale and confidence of the American soldier were surging to new highs. Even with the end nowhere in sight, some soldiers were already beginning to think about what they would do when the war was over. "I am very anxious to get back into G-d's own country, the state of Vermont, where I intend to settle down and pursue the course of life along the agricultural lines."[93] Private First Class (PFC) Russell Whitney, despite the vague outlook for the war in the early summer, which he likened to a "Chinese puzzle;"[94] had already made up his mind he was going to become a farmer once the war ended and he was out of the army. At the time he was writing this letter (middle of June), the AEF was very much in the thick of the fighting, having secured Cantigny and battling for control of Chateau-Thierry and Belleau Wood, in the hopes of getting "a chance to punch the Kaiser's nose."[95] After 30 hours of intense fighting, the German forces fell back from Chateau-Thierry on June 1, 1918; and from Belleau Wood after 96 hours on June 4, 1918. The American forces had provided the necessary reinforcements to tip the balance of the war in the favor of the Allies.[96]

Chateau-Thierry and Belleau Wood were the two locations along the Marne River where the U.S. 2nd and 3rd Infantry Divisions became the two of the first Allied Divisions to halt and repulse the westward German advance during the war. It marked the first time the German march towards Paris had been stopped since the American divisions came in support of the French troops, who had until early June 1918, been falling back towards Paris and away from the advancing Germans. With their troop lines established behind the French, the American Expeditionary Force was finally able to turn the tide of the war completely in the Allies' favor, as they repulsed several German counterattacks, while completely thwarting Germany's final attempt to cross the Marne on the way to Paris. By the middle of July, the Allies had the Germans in a full retreat back across France and Belgium towards Berlin, their capital city.

Back in Springfield, the city was becoming more modernized, as gas pipes and sidewalks were being laid down and installed around the city during the month of June. Gladys and Edna were also beginning to do some canning again now that their gardens were beginning to bear the bounty of summer fruits and vegetables; and in their weekly letters, they would again compare notes on how much, and of what, each of them canned the previous week. Even though there were a couple of frosty June mornings, the gardens continued to produce an abundant amount of food; with strawberries and cherries being the two major fruits which were getting canned at this time. By this time, the sugar rationing system had been nearly perfected with each family being allowed to purchase a maximum of two pounds of sugar per person per month. Also, nothing was going to stop the annual July 4th celebrations which occurred in many cities and towns across the country.

Having finally seen some battle action at places like Cantigny, Belleau Wood and Chateau-Thierry, the soldiers now had all kinds of new experiences and stories with which to fill their letters and by the middle of July (July 18th), some of these letters written by the boys from Springfield began to find their way into the local newspaper. "I have been up to the front and under fire and have seen all there was to see of war… But I saw some sights I shall never forget. I saw a gun and a crew get struck by a German shell and blown to pieces; saw a plane brought down; was bombarded twice while on the road at night."[97] These are the recollections of Sergeant C.P. Bacon, who was in charge of delivering the ammunition to some of the big guns, like the Howitzer, also known as the "Big 155", before and during the Battle of Chateau-Thierry. His letter here was one of the first to be published in the *Springfield Reporter* which included some very vivid descriptions of a World War One battlefield. Sergeant Bacon's letter tells of how the American troops were under pretty regular shelling from the Germans and of the conditions they faced as he and his men drove their ammunition truck to and from the gun placements. It had to be a nerve racking experience for Sergeant Bacon and his men because since their truck was loaded with shells, they wouldn't have had much of a chance of escaping had a German shell landed anywhere near their truck and its explosive cargo. Bacon goes on to mention how many of the French troops in their area, thought he and his Yankee comrades were crazy to unload their truck so close to the guns themselves.

As the American Expeditionary Force began to take on a more active role in the war effort in France during the summer of 1918, the soldiers' letters were constantly filled with stories about their battle experiences and accomplishments. However, even though their families and fellow Americans back on the homefront weren't shooting at an enemy army or winning battles in the field, didn't mean that they had nothing to brag about when it came to contributing to a successful war effort. On June 28, 1918, people all over the United States embarked on a campaign to sell $2,000,000,000 of War Savings Stamps. Like the Liberty Bonds, the money raised from the sale of these stamps would go to fund the war effort as well as to help aid the Red Cross. Each state had a quota when it came to how much money in war stamps, they wanted their people to buy and Vermont's was $7,365,200.[98] This, along with several successful Liberty Bond campaigns and consistent contributions to the Red Cross, which came in the form of pajamas and other items needed in the V.A.D. hospitals, were what American civilians could boast about when it came to helping the war effort. The soldiers were always very appreciative of these civilian efforts and very often took the time, in their letters, to praise the contributions the people of their hometown made to the war effort.

PFC Russell Whitney in his letter of July 4th took the time to praise his hometown of Springfield and everything it had done for the war effort. "I was quite pleased to learn how well Springfield is doing its bit toward downing Autocracy by contributing the fine sum of over $300,000 to the Liberty Loan campaign."[99] Along with being the home to several major machine companies which helped produce many of the shells the American guns fired, it was also the home of a very generous populous when it came to contributing to organizations like the Red Cross and buying Liberty Loans. According to ads in the *Springfield Reporter*, the $300,000 in Liberty Loans, which the people of Springfield purchased, was the highest of any city or town in Vermont. As a result of this, PFC Whitney exclaims, "(This contribution) shows that the hearts of the people of our great little town are in the right place, but also helps to demonstrate the prosperity of Springfield's inhabitants,"[100] PFC Whitney, like every other person from Springfield, could not have been any prouder of his town's contributions to helping the Allies defeat the Germans and ensure a swift end to the Great War.

As the summer rolled into the fall, the lives of the people of Springfield began to settle down and return to normal. In August 1918, Lawrence and Gladys were able to take a couple trips to places like White River Junction and Lake Sunapee, to do a little sightseeing; something they hadn't done much of since the United States entered the war back in April 1917. Other than that, Gladys spent most of her time either canning tomatoes and cucumbers or renewing an old hobby playing the piano. She also had begun to sell some of what she was canning to some of her neighbors in order to pick up a little side cash. She also spent a fair amount of time with her daughter, Evelyn, who was growing up fast and eating even faster; as Lawrence continued to put in long hours at Bryant for the remainder of the war. Interestingly though, there are no letters written by Gladys between early July and late August, something of which she was never apologetic for either. Reasonable speculation for the lack of letters at this time is that maybe during this time she was visiting her sister, Edna, in Feeding Hills, MA and as such there was no reason to write or perhaps these few letters got lost at some point. Since there is no indication of any unusual activity taking place on either side of the given time period, I have concluded that the most probable reason for the lack of letters between Gladys and Edna at this time would be the first explanation; being she was with her family in Feeding Hills and therefore didn't need to write to them at that time. However, as to why there are no letters at this time between Gladys and Lawrence is most likely the second explanation; which is they were lost or inadvertently discarded at some later date. In both cases, another reason for the lack of letter writing could be because the summer of 1918 was a very busy time for everyone. Between Lawrence's increased hours at the machine shop due to the war and with Edna and Gladys having the tobacco harvest, among the other farm chores, to attend to in Feeding Hills, MA; the activity of writing letters may have just taken a back seat for a few weeks that summer.

Chapter 7

The Final Push

In August 1918, the Allies were ready to make their final push against Germany and the other Axis Powers by closing in on them from all directions – west, east and south. The plan of attack, which was adopted by the Allies, was developed by Field Marshal Douglas Haig, the commander of the British Expeditionary Force (BEF) and came to be known as the Hundred Days Offensive. The Allies went into action on August 8th, when they surprised the Germans at Amiens (France) and by the end of the day had created a 15 mile wide gap in the German Lines while German losses were estimated to be about 30,000 including 17,000 prisoners. Even though the territorial gains by the Allies were minimal, Haig pushed his men on through to Somme and then to Albert, which was recaptured on August 22nd. By the beginning of September, the Allies had pushed the Germans back 34 miles to the Hindenburg Line, which stretched across Western Belgium and Northeast France, and marked the farthest permanent western positions of Germany's defensive front. On September 29, 1918, a U.S. led attack broke through the German Forces along the Hindenburg Line and finally drove them into a full retreat back towards Berlin and the heart of Germany.[101]

On September 12th, the American Expeditionary Force (AEF) surrounded the Germans at St. Mihiel, closing in from Verdun in the north and from Nancy and Luneville in the south. By the next morning, the German troops at St. Mihiel had been crushed and were pushed even further back. The attack was so quick and so successful, General John Pershing began to pull back some of his men in preparation for the "Meuse-Argonne Offensive"; which was planned by AEF Colonel George Marshall, who would later become the U.S. Army's Chief-of-Staff during World War Two. The objective of this offensive was to capture the rail station in Sedan, France which would cut the German Army off from any supplies and reinforcements it might need to continue fighting. From September 26th to October 17th, the AEF won battles at Somme-Py (Sept. 26th), Saint-Thierry (Sept. 30th), GrandPre (Oct. 16th) and Montfaucon (Oct. 17th) as they surged through the Argonne Forest towards Sedan. Small as they were, these American attacks were writing on the wall for the German High Command. On other fronts of the war, the British and Australian Forces managed to capture Constantinople, Damascus and Aleppo from the Ottoman-Turks which would lead to their surrender on October 30th; while the Italians raced into Austria across the Piave line, causing the Austrian forces to surrender on November 3rd.

The formal fighting between the Allies and the Central Powers came to an abrupt end on Thursday, November 7, 1918, when American and French troops captured the rail station in Sedan and secured the surrounding areas, thus cutting off the German supply lines and hence their ability to keep on fighting. That evening at approximately 9:15pm local time, a German delegation led by Matthias Erzberger approached the Allied lines near Haudroy, France in cars, each of which had been adorned with a white flag, a traditional symbol of peace and surrender. There, they were met by men of the French Army's 171st Infantry Regiment, who after verifying the delegates' identifications and credentials, blindfolded them before proceeding to take them to the Chateau Francfort in the Compiegne Forest, about eighty miles from Haudroy. There, Erzberger, General Detlev von Winterfeldt, Count Alfred von Oberndoff, Captain Ernst von Salow, General von Grunnel and the other five delegates spent the night, before being received by Marshal Foch the following morning. The next day at 9:00am French time, the delegation was brought to Rethondes, where Marshal Foch awaited them aboard his personal train in a railroad car which had been converted into a conference room. Once everyone was situated, the negotiations commenced with Marshal Foch supplying the Germans with a very specific list of demands which the Allies expected to be met in order for the war to reach its final conclusion.[102] Two hours later and having read aloud the armistice stipulations in minute detail, Foch told Erzberger and his fellow delegates that the German Government had seventy-two hours to either accept or reject these terms, with a strict deadline of Monday, November 11th at 11:00am French time.[103]

When the news of the end of the fighting in France reached the American Homefront in the early afternoon of November 7th, dozens of American cities and towns erupted into numerous impromptu celebrations, many of which lasted the remainder of the daylight hours, if not longer. According to Gladys, the celebration in Springfield, Vermont lasted well into the evening local time and was highlighted by the incessant ringing of church bells and blowing of shop whistles.[104] As the people of Springfield celebrated the end of the combat in Europe, many were also rejoicing in the realization that their friends and loved ones overseas would soon be back home, maybe even in time to celebrate the holidays in their own homes for the first time in two years. However, as exciting as this initial celebration was, it was just a prelude of what was to come four days later, following Germany's signing of the Armistice on November 11th.

The Armistice itself was signed at 5:00am French time and was designated to go into effect, six hours later at 11:00am French time, which worked out to be the 11th hour of the 11th day of the 11th month of the year or 6:00am Eastern standard time (EST). The signing of the Armistice brought the Great War to its official conclusion well ahead of anyone's original predictions, military or civilian. The United States had managed to turn the tide of the war and defeat Germany in just 168 short days, which given the limited success of the Allied forces before the arrival of American troops is probably safe to assume. General Pershing summed up the American impact on the war as follows, "It was this spirit of determination animating every American soldier that made it impossible for the enemy to maintain the struggle;"[105] and the same could be said for each and every American civilian as well. Without the invaluable contributions of civilians such as Lawrence Reed whose production in the factories kept the soldiers well-armed and supplied, the success of the

American troops in turning the tide of the war against the Germans would not have been as swift or as decisive as it was.

Even though the official terms of the Armistice would not be made known to the general public until the following year, the Associated Press issued an unofficial outline of the terms shortly after the Armistice's signing was announced by the U.S. State Department, at 2:45am EST on the morning of November 11th,[106] [107] According to the Associated Press's outline, the terms of the Armistice required Germany to remove, disarm and demobilize all of their armies and naval forces, while under the strict supervision of an Allied occupation force comprised of soldiers and sailors from the United States and the other Allied nations; such as the United Kingdom and France.[108] In the hopes of avoiding and preventing the rise of any new hostilities on the part of the German people or military, the Allies stationed men and supplies in every strategic German city and port as a deterrent to any unprovoked postwar conflicts.[109] As part of the disarmament of its military, Germany was also required to surrender a portion of its navy, including a yet unknown number of submarines.[110] Lastly, Germany was required to release any Allied military and civilian personnel who were currently being held as prisoners-of-war (POWs), without any expectation of the Allied Governments providing any similar reciprocating action.[111] While the Armistice ended the fighting and brought a formal ceasefire to the hostilities, the state of war between Germany and the Allies dragged on for another seven months, while the terms of a peace treaty were negotiated at the Paris Peace Conference. The peace treaty, known as the Treaty of Versailles was formally signed on June 28, 1919.[112] Interestingly though, the United States was the only Allied power to never ratify the Treaty of Versailles, even though there was tremendous public pressure on the House of Representatives and Senate to do so.[113] The United States did not formally end its involvement in World War One until July 2, 1921 when then President Warren G. Harding signed into law, the Knox-Porter Resolution, having been passed by both houses of Congress the previous day.[114] The Knox-Porter Resolution was a separate peace treaty between the United States and Germany, which came out of a special session of Congress which

President Harding had called for in April 1921. The United States refused to ratify the Treaty of Versailles because of its strong opposition to the League of Nations and its differing views regarding the treaty's reparations settlement.[115]

With the signing of the Armistice on November 11th, the Great War had come to a more formal, diplomatic end; which meant when dawn broke that morning there were additional celebrations which kicked off in many cities and towns across the United States. Many of which were very similar to those which had taken place four days earlier when the last of the formal fighting reached its conclusion. For instance, in Springfield, their celebration kicked off at 7:30am, when all the church bells and shop whistles throughout the town all began to chime and whistle. At 9:00am, all the men quit work for the day and ran to watch the parade and rally, which highlighted the festivities in Springfield that day. Those who didn't actively participate in the parade by doing things such as riding the many homemade floats, which many of the local companies had built for the parade, either stood on street corners or found some other safe vantage point which gave them a good view of all the local festivities; which lasted the majority of the day. Amidst all the revelry and merriment which highlighted these festivities, Gladys was just thankful that she and her family managed to complete all her errands that day, while Armistice celebrations were taking place in both Springfield, as well as in the nearby town of Bellows Falls, Vermont, which was having its celebration when the Reeds arrived there in the middle of the afternoon.[116] [117]

Causes of the War

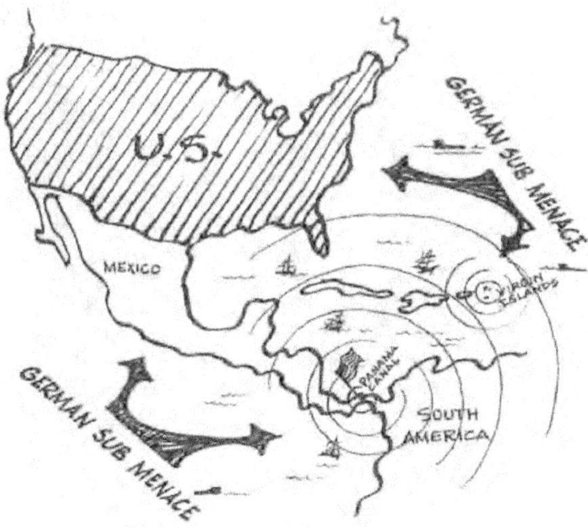

The Zimmermann Telegram text (reproduced as image):

CANCELED
1-8-58
State Dept.

TELEGRAM RECEIVED.

FROM 2nd from London # 5747.

"We intend to begin on the first of February unrestricted submarine warfare. We shall endeavor in spite of this to keep the United States of America neutral. In the event of this not succeeding, we make Mexico a proposal of alliance on the following basis: make war together, make peace together, generous financial support and an understanding on our part that Mexico is to reconquer the lost territory in Texas, New Mexico, and Arizona. The settlement in detail is left to you. You will inform the President of the above most secretly as soon as the outbreak of war with the United States of America is certain and add the suggestion that he should, on his own initiative, invite Japan to immediate adherence and at the same time mediate between Japan and ourselves. Please call the President's attention to the fact that the ruthless employment of our submarines now offers the prospect of compelling England in a few months to make peace." Signed, ZIMMERMANN.

The Zimmermann Telegram

Unrestricted Submarine Warfare

World War One Era Artifacts
(Civilian and Military)

Souvenir Postcards of
Washington, D.C.

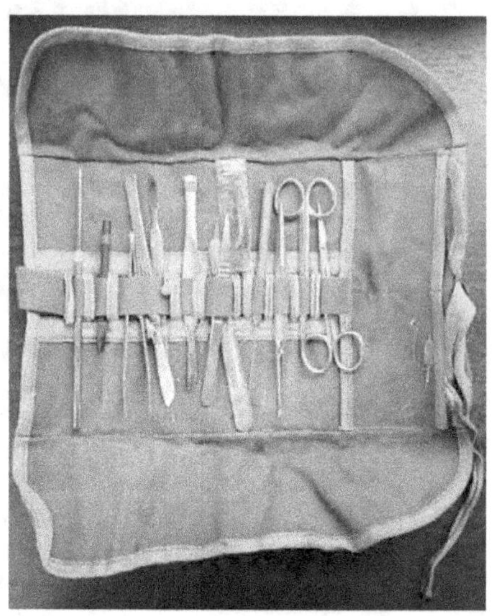

Soldier's Medical Kit

U.S.C.E. Compass

Soldier's Lighter

Company K Sendoff - 1917

Armistice Day Celebrations:
Parade November 11, 1918

WOMEN WAR WORKERS
J. & L. McH. Co.
— 100 —

CUSTOM TAILOR

Armistice Day Celebrations: Rally
November 11, 1918

Machine Shop – Armistice Day

World War One Era Ceremonial American Flag

Chapter 8

Thanksgiving on the Homefront

About the only downside to the war ending was the effect it had on people like Lawrence, whose job was partially dependent on the war; given the soldiers' needs for both bullets and other larger ammunition shells. The end of the fighting meant the United States Military was already in the process of cancelling orders for such supplies; which at least temporarily cut down the amount of work done in the shop, until it was able to repurpose its operations to producing the products it had been making before the war, such as the chucking grinders.[118] However, it was very tough to be depressed for any reason on such a joyous day, especially since the Armistice celebrations put many people into high spirits; feelings which, for many, probably lasted through the remainder of the year, given the proximity of the war's end to both Thanksgiving and the upcoming holiday season.[119] Even though the war had just come to an end and millions of Americans were now in the process of getting ready for Thanksgiving, President Wilson, in his Thanksgiving Day Proclamation, which was issued on November 16, 1918, asked the American people to take some time this Thanksgiving to: one, remember all the men and women who sacrificed so much to insure an Allied victory, and two, remember how the American people united both in their country's defense and later in celebration of the aforementioned Allied victory. In this proclamation, which was printed in newspapers across the country the following day,[120] Wilson emphasized the rationale for why everyone should be especially appreciative and thankful this year. "Complete victory has brought us not just peace alone, but the confident promise of a new day as well… We have cause for such rejoicing as revives and strengthens in us, in which our hearts take new courage and look forward with new hope to new and greater duties."[121] After four years of uncertainty, which included nineteen months of active involvement in the Great War, Wilson's message must have been echoing in the minds and thoughts of all American families such as the Reeds, whose loved ones had contributed to the war effort; whether as soldiers overseas or in Lawrence's case, back on the homefront, where the efforts of he, his fellow machinists and the many other skilled laborers helped ensure the success of the soldiers overseas by keeping them well armed and supplied. It is safe to assume that many Americans were probably extra thankful and reflective that year on Thanksgiving as they gathered with friends and family to enjoy each other's company, while partaking in the many delicacies of the Thanksgiving table.[122]

Given the United States Military's demand for certain types of food, such as sugar, as they attempted to keep the soldiers and sailors well fed while on the front lines, one might think that some of the traditional Thanksgiving foods which Americans knew so well might have been difficult to make due to the lack of certain key ingredients. However, given the ingenuity of Americans to come up with substitutions for those key ingredients, such as maple syrup in the place   of sugar, the Thanksgiving table of 1918 did not suffer as much as it could have.

In the case of the Reed and Steere Families, Thanksgiving in 1918 was spent in Feeding Hills, MA at the home of Howard and Edna Steere, Gladys's older brother and sister who still lived on the family farm, which all three of them had grown up on. For a family with very simple roots and backgrounds, in terms of means and lifestyle, the Reed/Steere clan was able to put on quite a spread when it came to Thanksgiving. The Thanksgiving meal enjoyed by the Reeds and Steeres in 1918 was highlighted by a fresh turkey which had been slaughtered and dressed the previous day and was baked with a bread stuffing along with numerous side dishes. The hot side dishes included three types of mashed vegetables – white potatoes, butternut squash and turnips which were most likely rutabagas. There were also: creamed onions, giblet gravy, bread, rolls and butter, and two kinds of cranberry sauce – whole berry and jellied. Prior to the main meal, there was also: cheese, crackers, olives, pickles, grapes, celery and a bowl of mixed nuts to munch on. As Methodists and strict followers of its doctrine, there was not a drop of alcohol to be found in the Steere household in Feeding Hills. So, unlike some Thanksgiving dinners where the preferred drink was wine, coffee was the drink of choice for the Reed and Steere Families. The rationale for Methodists' abstinence from wine and other intoxicating liquors was a fear of its consumption leading to sin, crime and immoral behavior.[123] [124] The Methodist doctrine tells its members to abstain from consuming any wine or "spirituous liquor, no dram of any kind, unless prescribed by a physician,"[125] something which Lawrence swore to later in life, when he was known to consume two teaspoons of whiskey on nights he had trouble getting to sleep, but only after the remedy was prescribed to him by his doctor. Finally, for dessert, three types of pie were served – apple, squash (not pumpkin) and mince. Like many Americans, Wilson's message for the holiday was probably very much on the minds of the Reed and Steere Families as they prepared and enjoyed their Thanksgiving dinner that year. His words provided the American people with a gentle reminder to reflect on and be thankful for the war's conclusion and for the new era of worldwide peace and stability which would hopefully become a reality in the years to come; as families in both Europe and North America sought to rebuild and return to the lives and livelihoods they had known before the Great War came to or threatened their shores.

Chapter 9

The Flu: A New War

However, even though the fighting in Europe had ceased and many American families could now sit down for their Thanksgiving meals with a sense of hope and peace, and the anticipation of their loved ones in uniform coming home in the upcoming weeks and months, there was another new kind of war which had begun to brew and was poised to impact many of these same households. One of the things which would make this new war so far reaching is that the very soldiers Americans were looking forward to welcoming home would end up being one of the primary conduits which brought the new battle to the shores of North America.

Just as the United States was preparing to turn the tide of the war against the Germans, a strain of flu was beginning to take root in cities and towns all over Western Europe. On May 22, 1918, the flu made headlines in Madrid's *ABC Newspaper*, right in the middle of the Fiesta de San Isidro, a local holiday which honors the city's patron saint, Isidro Labrador, who in the twelfth century had the gift of locating sources of water in times of need.[126] The feast which takes place around May 15th each year and is known for its parties called verbenas, typically draws hundreds of people to the city of Madrid and the surrounding villages. Even though, this strain of influenza which would come to be known as the "Spanish Flu" got some of its first major publicity in Spain, many experts today believe that the epidemic actually originated in France and was in turn brought to Spain via the railroad by migrant Spanish and Portuguese workers; who regularly commuted to and from villages in

France where they were doing the work usually done by the French men who at the time were on the front lines of battle. However, the flu did not limit its victims to those of the middle and lower classes, as even Spain's leader, King Alfonso XIII, had a case of the flu during the epidemic's first phase; which lasted from May to July 1918.

With the hope that avoiding as much human contact as possible would make them less likely to contract the flu, many Spaniards began to stay at home and indoors most of time. By doing this, some hoped that the lack of contact would keep the virus from spreading any further than it already had, while isolating those who had already contracted the disease from those who were still healthy. As a result, many Spaniards did not go into work, which in turn led to the temporary closure of some public services such as the post office, the telegraph and the banks. Fortunately, there were very few fatal cases during the early months of the epidemic – about 4 per 100,000 cases, and by July 1918, the flu had all but disappeared. However, this respite was short-lived as cases began to reappear in France, Spain and Portugal by the beginning of September 1918. This second phase of the epidemic, which had a much higher rate of fatal cases – about 50 per 100,000 cases, lasted until December 1918 and very briefly shut down many schools and universities in the region.

In order to keep the influenza from spreading as rapidly, strict infection measures were implemented with regards to those workers who travelled between France and the Iberian Peninsula on a regular basis. In the previous months, the workers were allowed to get off the trains at any of the station stops in order to walk around, get a bite to eat, etc. so long as they returned to train when it was time to leave. However, in an attempt to keep the influenza in check, starting in September 1918, the workers now had to remain on the train at all times until they each reached the station in their hometown. The hope here was that by limiting the contact the workers had with the local townspeople this would, in turn, limit the number of new influenza cases. However, given the increasing rates of both cases and fatalities as the epidemic went on, the effectiveness of these influenza control measures were only marginally helpful, if they were at all. The influenza epidemic would linger in

Western Europe for another six months until June 1919, by which time the Armistice had been signed and the majority of American soldiers had returned home.

Just as the migrant Spanish and Portuguese workers were responsible for helping the influenza spread through Western Europe by contracting it and then bringing it to their hometowns as they commuted to and from France; the American soldiers inadvertently played a similar role when they brought the influenza home to their families back in the United States, particularly in the states along the Atlantic coast. As the United States Army amassed and prepared its forces for battle, starting in the summer of 1917, it did so in camps which were very often in close proximity to some of the local villages in Central and Southern France. The soldiers were also known to mingle with the locals and very often frequented the local establishments in the area. This constant contact, with the local French, created many more opportunities for the soldiers to not only contract influenza, but to also spread it around. Not only did the soldiers spread it to each other, both in their camps as well as on the ships which were transporting sick and wounded men back to the United States, but also to the people back home when they arrived back in the United States.

Even though the flu did not make headlines in Europe until May 1918, it is pretty clear that it had already been around for at least a few months, given that the first case of the flu in the United States was a soldier who had just returned from Europe to Fort Riley, Kansas on March 11, 1918. However, like in Europe, the first wave of the influenza in the United States was also short-lived with mostly mild cases reported along with very few fatalities. However, by September 1918, the influenza virus had mutated and a second, more intense wave of the disease, was gaining steam and was about to hit Americans both at home and abroad; with much greater consequences, including higher rates of both fatalities as well as overall cases.[127] At the same time, the epidemic was in the process of becoming a worldwide issue with new pockets of the mutated virus appearing on three continents practically simultaneously: in Freetown, Sierra Leone (Africa), Brest, Belgium (Europe) and Boston, Massachusetts (North America).[128] However, it is still unclear whether all these pockets of the disease were the product of one mutation of the influenza virus or three different mutations of the virus which all took place at the same time.[129]

For the most part, the influenza was primarily ignored by authorities back in the United States, which can probably be attributed to the rather mild nature of the epidemic's first wave in the late spring and early summer of 1918. Once the second wave of the epidemic struck in the late summer though, everyone including the government, began to take notice of the severity of the problems the epidemic was causing. Much of this sudden awareness can be attributed to the increase of the severity of the second wave as opposed to that of the first wave of the influenza. Unfortunately, very few places took any precautionary measures in efforts to protect the local citizens; particularly with the number of armed forces personnel who had come down with influenza and were returning home where they would end up spreading it to their families and friends. Other things which took people's attention away from dealing with the epidemic and its consequences, particularly in the Boston area, included the Senate vote on women's suffrage, the trial of Eugene Debs, the Russian Revolution, [130] and the 1918 World Series victory by the Boston Red Sox; a feat this organization would not accomplish for the next 86 years.

Since the first case of influenza reported in the United States was located at a military base, this was where the U.S. Government first focused the attention of their efforts to attempt to control and contain the spread of the virus. However, given the lack of an organized network of public health departments on the federal, state and local levels, it was very difficult to ever get enough existing data to develop a clear picture of the extent of the epidemic in terms of areas affected and the number of known cases.[131] This lack of communication also meant that early on in the epidemic, very few places in the United States knew what to do about the flu or what this particular strain even was. In many cases those who perished in the epidemic were believed to have been killed by pneumonia, which would set in after the flu had taken a taxing toll on their immune systems, which made them more susceptible and vulnerable to a more debilitating disease such as pneumonia. According to historian Alfred Crosby, Jr., another thing which made the 1918 Influenza Epidemic so tough for those trying to treat it was the common medical knowledge of the time which said that the age groups who were most likely to be impacted the most by flu and pneumonia were those who were very young, such as infants and little kids, or very old, such as elderly senior citizens. However, the highest rate of cases of this strain of flu, in particular fatal cases, was actually found in the 20 to 29 age bracket.[132] The high rates of fatalities in this age group was particularly alarming and difficult for people to understand, especially since men of a similar age were perishing at an equally rapid rate from wounds suffered on the battlefield as World War One raged across Western Europe. With the war on the forefront of people's minds in the spring and summer of 1918, the flu did not receive any better coverage in Europe as compared to the United States. The first cases of the flu were found amongst the men of the British Expeditionary Force (BEF) and German troops in April; and amongst the French forces the following month. The most hard hit country was still Spain, with over eight million cases by the end June, which gave this strain of flu its famous nickname of "Spanish Influenza."[133]

Like in Europe, the first wave of the Spanish Influenza in the United States ended after a couple months with minimal impact and very few fatal cases. However, when the second wave of the disease, which is believed to have begun in Boston, Massachusetts on August 27, 1918, arose; it did so with remarkable speed as far as the total area impacted and the overall number of known cases, fatal and otherwise. Just as in March, the first reported case of the flu in the epidemic's second wave was an American serviceman, in this case a sailor who reported to the sick bay at Commonwealth Pier in Boston on the aforementioned August 27th.[134] Within two weeks of this first case, over 2,000 additional naval officers and sailors in the area had also contracted the disease.[135] Despite the rapid rate of newly reported cases, the local and state governments of the region did very little, if anything to warn or protect their citizens from the epidemic. The local and state government officials in Boston and Massachusetts did not give the flu the concern it warranted as they were preoccupied with making sure all the necessary war supplies made it out to sea and over to the soldiers in Europe in a timely manner. They also were blinded by the city's most recent health report; which said that the overall health of the local population was better than it had been in several years, as was indicated by a decreased death rate coupled with a spike in population growth.[136] As such, the flu's second wave received very little attention when there were still opportunities to curb its spread.

It took a mere, very short thirty-three days for the second wave of Spanish Influenza to spread across the United States from the Atlantic to the Pacific coasts and in the process leaving very few areas untouched in its wake. After getting a foothold in Boston in late August, the flu had reached all portions of Eastern Massachusetts by September 14th, the entire Atlantic coastline from Maine to Virginia by September 21st and all areas of the Atlantic States by September 28th. By October 5th and shortly thereafter, the flu had spread to all the major population areas in the United States; followed shortly thereafter by all the rural and more isolated regions of the country. By October 1918, the lives of the majority of Americans had in some way been impacted by the flu epidemic, either by having the disease or knowing someone else whose life had been impacted as such. It wasn't until cases of influenza began to be reported in army and navy bases from Boston and Washington, D.C. to San Francisco, California and Puget Sound, Washington; that the United States Government finally realized they could no longer ignore the flu.[137] According to Crosby, by the summer of 1918, the government came to the realization there was an issue on their own shores which deserved as much or more priority than what was going on overseas.[138]

Chapter 10
Springfield: A Case of Two Wars

It cannot be overstated just how little the American populous knew about the Spanish Influenza and its impacts, when there was still some time to put preventative measures in place to keep the disease from spreading as much as it did. In some cases, people didn't become aware of it until they either caught it themselves or learned of a friend or family member who had gotten it. For instance, even though, Springfield, Vermont is barely one hundred miles northwest of Boston, the suggested epicenter of the flu's second wave in the United States; the local newspaper, the *Springfield Reporter*, made no reference to the disease until the end of September 1918. The first mention of "Spanish Influenza" in the *Springfield Reporter* can be found in the September 26, 1918 edition of the paper, when the Red Cross sent out a telegram to many towns and cities in Windsor County, Vermont asking if people would assist them by knitting pajamas for the influenza victims who were beginning to fill up army hospitals and elsewhere.[139] By making reference to the flu epidemic the local media had made the people of Springfield very aware of Spanish Influenza and what its impacts were. In the hopes of avoiding catching the disease, the majority of the local townspeople began to stay indoors and seclude themselves in their homes; as much as possible, while many of the shops and services in town also ceased to function, which according to one local, turned Springfield into a virtual ghost town.

Over the next six months (October 1918 – April 1919), the people of Springfield, would for the most part, not leave their homes for fear of catching the flu. As a result, many of the shops, entertainment and other services in town would, in turn, shut down as well, turning the city into a virtual ghost town. For the most part, the most common sights on the streets were the doctors whose job it was to tend to the ailing flu victims in the many homes around town. Given the lack of activity around town, the Armistice celebration on November 11, 1918 must have seemed like a breath of fresh air for many people as the townspeople gathered to celebrate the end of the war. One of the few industries in Springfield which kept its shops active, despite the impacts and dangers of the flu epidemic, were the machine shops, which had government contracts which still needed to be honored, even if it meant operating with a shorthanded workforce on account of the disease's presence in Springfield and the surrounding region. As such, men such as Lawrence Reed were still going to work every day in order to keep the soldiers armed and supplied, even if it meant taking a chance of contracting the influenza virus. Given the widespread impact of the flu, it is also easy to understand how once the virus arrived in town, the contents of people's conversations and letters during this time became dominated by the Spanish Influenza and how it was impacting people on a daily basis.

The first mention of the Spanish Influenza in the correspondence which Gladys Reed had with her sister, Edna Steere, who lived in Feeding Hills, Massachusetts, can be found in Gladys's letter to Edna, dated October 2, 1918. As we have already seen during the earlier years of the war, a correspondence as complete and as vivid as that of the Steere (Reed) sisters can really paint a very accurate picture of what life was like for the common American at this time. It is personal insights and details such as those provided in these letters which show just how challenging and restricted people's lives became in light of the influenza outbreak. In the early days of the epidemic, the U.S. Government did very little to either warn their citizens about the flu or enact measures to help treat the victims and prevent it from spreading further. As such, many of the actions which people took to guard themselves from getting the flu and to treat those who had already caught it were constituted primarily on the local level and in some cases even on the personal level. On October 2nd, just as cases of the flu were beginning to become known in Springfield, Gladys wrote to Edna, "We all stay pretty close in our own quarters now-a-days on account of the Spanish Influenza. It is raging dreadfully here, especially in the Polish sections."[140] As mentioned above, once cases of the flu began to become commonplace and common knowledge in towns such as Springfield, a lot of people began to stay indoors in the hopes of avoiding catching the disease. This, along with the many shops and services which ceased to function in Springfield, had to have created a very circumscribed and boring lifestyle for the Reeds and the many other families in the Springfield area.

Starting with her letter of October 2nd, Gladys very frequently would provide a "casualty list" within the text of each letter she wrote to her sister, Edna. On this list, she would go through as many flu victims as she was aware of and what the current medical status of each victim was. In this first "flu letter", Gladys's list includes eight victims, including the wife of their landlord in Springfield, Mrs. Dashner, and the man who worked at Bryant Chucking Grinder Company at the station next to Lawrence's. What is very intriguing about this first list of cases is that two of the victims on this list were actually referenced to by Gladys in her previous two letters to Edna. For both of these victims, Gladys makes it very clear that while local doctors had some ideas about what these two people might have, they really didn't know what they were dealing with. On September 17th, Gladys writes to Edna, "Mr. Hobson's son (George) is in the hospital with typhoid fever, I guess. They don't seem to be sure just what does ail him but I guess they call it that. He is very sick."[141] What made diagnosing patients with the Spanish flu so difficult in the beginning was that the symptoms the disease exhibited were very similar to those of a common cold, a less aggressive strand of the flu or other things such as typhoid fever. Some of the most common symptoms of all these diseases include a high fever, sore throat, fatigue and muscle aches.[142] What separated the Spanish Influenza from these other diseases, and initially made it difficult to diagnose and successfully treat for doctors, was the way it would very quickly transition into pneumonia in a fair number of the victims, when the virus spread to their lungs.[143] In the majority of the cases where the virus turned into pneumonia, it would happen so quickly and so suddenly that, more often than not, the patient would be killed by the pneumonia before the disease could be successfully treated or even discovered. However, Mr. Hobson's son was not the only person from Springfield who had become infected by the epidemic before the local townspeople had ever heard the term "Spanish Influenza".

On September 24th, Gladys tells Edna that their landlord's wife, Mrs. Dashner, who lived in the apartment above the one the Reeds lived in, was feeling better from something which ailed her, but that she continued to be very fatigued most of the time.[144] Fortunately for Mrs. Dashner, she was able to recover from this mysterious ailment, which given the fact that she had previously complained of fatigue, seems to suggest that her mystery illness was Spanish Influenza. What is even more incredible is how all the Reeds managed to avoid catching the flu at this time especially when they lived in such close proximity to the Dashners. The Reeds' worry of contracting the influenza was most likely fueled by the fact that they had a six month old baby in the house and being in their early twenties, both Lawrence and Gladys had to have been especially concerned for themselves as well, since that was the age bracket (20-29) which was most devastated by the epidemic.

Along with Mrs. Dashner and the Hobson boy, Gladys's casualty list in her October 2nd letter to Edna lists an additional six people who had contracted the flu virus and either had it, were not doing well, had been killed by it or were recovering from it. In many cases there was no way of knowing how one might fair once he or she had contracted the virus. In most cases, it was all a matter of how quickly pneumonia set in. If pneumonia set in, then most likely the person would not survive; otherwise there was always a prospect of recovery. Gladys then goes on to talk about just how quickly the virus has changed the goings on around town. "Everything is closed up here to keep it from spreading any more. It's the quietest place you ever saw – even the streets are nearly deserted."[145] Gladys here is remarking about some of the local measures the town took in the hopes of keeping the virus from spreading in the area. In order to do this, the majority of the local businesses shut down and, as a result, most people just stayed home all the time in order to avoid as much direct exposure to the disease as possible. According to Gladys, the only people who could be seen on the streets, at this point, were a few flu victims who had collapsed on the ground when venturing out at one time, the doctors who were circulating around the town to treat those who had contracted the virus and a few workmen, including Lawrence.[146]

Even though the majority of the town had shut its doors during the time the flu virus was in Springfield, life for the town's residents still had to proceed as close to normal as was possible. Since much of Springfield was shut down, Lawrence and Gladys found themselves going across the Connecticut River to Claremont, New Hampshire to run some of their errands. Even though the times were bleak, Lawrence and Gladys were probably able to keep their spirits up because of their young baby, Evelyn, who Gladys claimed was a constant source of laughter. However, it was very tough for Gladys to keep her spirits up at times, because she constantly worried about Lawrence catching the flu and bringing it home from work. Even though the flu virus was in town and many businesses were temporarily closed, one of the few industries which was still going strong during the epidemic was the machining industry. This was because the United States was still in the midst of the First World War and the flu virus was no excuse to temporarily stop furnishing the soldiers overseas with the supplies they needed to ensure a successful war effort. As a result, Lawrence and many of his fellow machinists continued to dutifully report to the factories every day during the epidemic, in order to ensure that the necessary number of bullets and other supplies were produced to fill the military's needs. What made Gladys particularly concerned for Lawrence was the man who worked the machine next to Lawrence's at Bryant had already contracted the flu virus; which for a couple days gave him constant and close exposure to the virus, until this man began staying home on account of being sick. As such, the factories were also not operating at full capacity since some of their employees, having contracted the disease, were not well enough to work. Even though some of the machinists were not able to come into work as a result of having contracted the flu, their fellow machinists were more than willing to pick up the slack by volunteering to work extra shifts and/or take on additional duties.

What a crisis situation, such as a war, an epidemic or, during the 1910s both, can cause people to do, is make them set aside some of their more personal values and beliefs in preference to those which can contribute more to the greater good by helping put an end to the given crisis at the time. As a man who had been raised with good Christian morals and values, Lawrence was someone who typically would not do work on the Sabbath. However, with the Allied forces making rapid gains across Western Europe in the summer and fall of 1918, the soldiers' need for supplies such as ammunition was an almost constant one. And with the Bryant factory already shorthanded due to the number of workers who were already laid up with the flu, Lawrence put his conflicting religious beliefs regarding doing work on the Sabbath aside and let his patriotism and love for his country motivate him to volunteer for the job of the factory's weekend night watchman. During which time he would maximize his productivity by continuing to work at his station throughout the night.[147] According to his wife Gladys, Lawrence "felt that he must accommodate them (his fellow workers) as much as he objects to Sunday work."[148] Lawrence, like many other Americans, both at home and abroad, was willing and able to make some sacrifices to do his part in the war effort, in order to ensure that there would be a United States of America for his children and grandchildren to enjoy.

Another one of the benefits, which going to work at the factory each day and contributing to the war effort did for Lawrence and his fellow workmen, was it gave each day some structure and balance while also providing a distraction from all the misery the war and even more so, the epidemic was causing many Americans to feel at this time. However, for people, such as their wives like Gladys, the same distractions were not as available to them, especially since many of them did not actually have jobs of their own at this time. Gladys for instance, spent many of her days in the fall of 1918 at home primarily with her daughter, Evelyn, while trying to stay busy by either doing chores or entertaining herself; either by knitting, playing the piano, keeping her daughter out of trouble or writing letters to friends and family. The last of these activities was the only way Gladys and many other Americans had of keeping in touch with their friends and family in other cities and towns because things such as cars and telephones were hardly commonplace at the time. Gladys's correspondence with her sister in Feeding Hills was done on a weekly, or sometimes a semiweekly basis, as they strove to keep each other informed about how they were making it through the epidemic and just what the overall situation was in their given localities; especially when the government and media at that time were not doing the best of jobs at keeping the populous informed about the impacts of the war and the epidemic on people's lives. As such, many of the countermeasures, which people took to combat the epidemic, were actually from the local and personal levels.

In an attempt to gather and isolate the victims of the flu epidemic from those who were still healthy, the town of Springfield, Vermont needed more space than their main hospital was able to offer. To fill this need, the town made arrangements with local businessman and President of the Vermont Snath Company, Walter M. White, to use his old home at 200 Clinton Street, as a temporary emergency hospital to house the growing number of victims of the epidemic.[149] White was able to do this, having just completed a new family house on Summer Street in Springfield.[150] According to Gladys, the house on Clinton Street provided the hospital with at least an additional fourteen rooms to house flu victims.[151] Just like in her October 2nd letter, Gladys caps her October 7th letter by giving a rundown of all the people, whom she knew, who had been or were being impacted by the influenza virus. She mentions their neighbors, who lived across the street from them, which was a Polish family, all of whom had been infected with the virus. On this list were also three of her friends, the Perrys and Mr. Deane, all of whom had either perished or were in poor condition as a result of contracting the disease.[152] The final group of people who Gladys mentions in her letter among those who had been infected by the virus also sheds some light on why Lawrence and some of   his fellow machinists were needed to volunteer for additional shifts in order to pick up the slack at the shop as a result of many of their colleagues being unable to come into work after having contracted the flu. According to Gladys, forty workers from the Bryant factory had contracted the disease, while three had already perished from it.[153] This high number of cases amongst the shop workers is probably what contributed to Gladys's concerns of Lawrence one day bringing the virus home from work. Finally, Gladys also urges Edna not to come and visit them while the epidemic is going on and ensures her they would not visit her if they weren't feeling well; just so they didn't risk spreading the virus around to her and her friends in the Feeding Hills area. At this point, one might be wondering why Gladys is taking so much time to tell her sister about these flu victims in her letters. Given that many of these aforementioned victims were friends and neighbors of the Reeds, it is reasonable to think that perhaps Gladys introduced many of these people to Edna during her visits to Springfield meaning she probably knew who many of these people were, as opposed to Gladys just providing a list of people who were victims of the epidemic, but also complete strangers as far as her sister was concerned.

Since there was no reliable medication or vaccine to combat the influenza at the time, doctors and private citizens began putting a lot of effort into searching for and experimenting with a myriad of curative and preventative measures; many of which could be considered in house or folk remedies. This was because many of these therapies had no basis in medical fact and were instead purely theoretical and speculative with a little bit of faith thrown in. At the same time the United States Public Health Service and public health officials began to tackle the challenge of educating the American people about the Spanish Influenza and what to do about it before it spread across the entire nation.[154] Fortunately, there were several companies and organizations who pitched in to help spread the word about the virus. The Red Cross, the Post Office, the Federal Railroad Administration and the Colgate Company all helped Surgeon General Rupert Blue distribute various pamphlets; with titles such as Spanish Influenza, Three-Day-Fever and The Flu, among others, each of which was designed to inform the American people about the influenza virus and its potential impacts.[155] According to Alfred Crosby, Jr., by the time the epidemic had subsided, the number of pamphlets which had been printed and distributed was so high, that if paper was a medicine, it would have smothered the disease long before the flu took as many victims as it did.[156] However, none of these actions did much to inhibit the spreading of the virus, nor did they stop people from trying to combat the disease itself, by experimenting with their own concoctions and elixirs, including the Reeds who confessed to using two of these very debatable homemade therapies.

The two homemade flu remedies, which Gladys confessed to using to Edna in her letter of October 13th, were a mixture of hydrogen peroxide, salt and water which she would gargle in her throat on a daily basis; and a sulfur bag,[157] a small sack of sulfur crystals which she would wear every time she had to go out of the house. It was believed that the fumes given off by the sulfur crystals would help fend off the flu and keep one from catching it.[158] However there were many other concoctions which many people, and some doctors, at the time believed would help fend off the influenza virus. Other elixirs, similar to the one Gladys used and recommended by some physicians, included chlorinated soda and a combination of sodium bicarbonate and boric acid. All of these rather suspect tonics were gargled in the same manner that the hydrogen peroxide and salt water mixture was.[159] While the people were out searching for a cure to the influenza, the American Public Health Association (APHA) was coming out with a number of more practical suggestions for people to use; which were intended to hopefully keep them from contracting the virus to begin with. These suggestions, some of which the APHA attempted to have made law included: no sharing of cups and utensils, a ban on sneezing and coughing in public, the encouragement to wash one's hands before meals and just a close watch on general hygiene overall.[160] They also warned people not to over exhaust their systems, while encouraging exposure to fresh air;[161] which was the complete opposite of some people's practice who, once the flu set in, didn't go outdoors any more than they absolutely had to.

Even though the vast majority of evidence regarding any positive impact these homemade remedies had in fighting the influenza was at best circumstantial, many people believed using them to at least try to battle the virus was better than putting their hopes of survival on time and luck. One of the most widely used folk remedies for the flu was onions in various forms. There are several stories of mothers whose children survived the epidemic by giving them a steady diet of onions in forms such as omelets, salads, soups and syrups. One girl was even said to have survived by being completely buried in raw onions for a period of three days. Other folk remedies, such as Sulphur and camphor, were used by those who had a dislike for onions.[162]

Although, the majority of remedies which people used to try to tackle the flu virus were of the homemade and anecdotal variety, there were a couple of medications which some people believed might help cure the flu because of its similarity to the ailments the drugs were initially designed to combat. One such drug was known as Formitol, which was developed by the E.L. Patch Company and came in a tablet form and was initially designed to be used to treat colds and sore throats.[163] The drug which is composed primarily of D-chiro Inositol; Methylfolate, a methylated from of Vitamin B_9; and Methylcobalamine, a methylated form of Vitamin B_{12};[164] was both prescribed by doctors and sold in local pharmacies, such as Magwire's Pharmacy in Springfield, Vermont.[165] The advertisement for Formitol as a flu treatment went as far as calling it "A Prophylactic against Spanish Influenza,"[166] which in layman's terms means a drug which would prevent or cure the flu. However, even though it was an actual drug, the helpfulness and success of the Formitol at treating the flu wasn't a whole lot better than the anecdotal success of the many folk remedies which people were also trying at this time.

Once the flu arrived in Springfield, it didn't waste much time spreading to the town's residents. By the second week in October, there were already close to 700 (692) known cases of Spanish Influenza according to the local newspaper, which amounted to about ten percent of the town's entire population of approximately 6,700! What became very clear was that once the flu got a foothold in a given area, while the number of cases initially would only be a few, the numbers would quickly begin to rise at a very rapid rate. As an example of this, while the *Springfield Reporter* reported approximately 700 cases in town in its October 10, 1918 issue, by the following week's issue, the number of cases it was reporting was almost 1200.[167] There was no person in town who was not in some way impacted by the flu epidemic; for even if they didn't contract the disease, they either knew someone who did or found themselves talking about it on a fairly regular basis. As Gladys put it in her letter of October 13th to Edna, "About all we hear about is influenza, so that's all there is to write."[168] She then goes on to detail some of the signs and impacts the disease was having on the town and its residents. According to Gladys, there were several tell-tale signs which identified a house as having a flu victim under its roof. The first of these signs was the constant sightings of the Red Cross nurse going to and from a home each day to tend to the sick individual(s). The other thing which identified a home as one with a flu victim inside of it was if all the windows were closed.

The flu had spread to so many people the town was forced to shut down its foundries on account of there not being enough healthy workers to run them at the time. Other people thought they could escape the flu virus if they just picked up and left town right then and there. Even though it was contrary to the way many people acted once the flu epidemic set in, the Reeds found the best medicine for combating the flu was just being outdoors, especially since the majority of those who were sick were those who had restricted themselves to their homes and didn't go anywhere.[169]

During the week of October 13th, the United States Public Health Service issued an official bulletin regarding the influenza epidemic, in the framework of an interview with Surgeon General Rupert Blue. This bulletin would be published in newspapers all across the country, from Vermont to California, and was probably one of the first notices which gave many Americans an exposure to what the Spanish Influenza was; assuming the disease had not already infiltrated their community. To begin with, Blue makes it very clear that the virus, which was responsible for the influenza outbreak as well as the place from where it originated were both still unknown to authorities at the time. One of the most widely accepted reasons for why the disease took on the name, "Spanish Influenza", was because it was the Spanish media which first reported that a disease of epidemic proportions was brewing in the spring of 1918.[170] Blue also warned Americans of the possibility of the disease perhaps taking on the name "American Influenza", should the disease become widespread throughout the country.[171] The bulletin then proceeded to answer some of the most common questions people had about influenza. It defined "Spanish Influenza" as a very contagious kind of a cold which was often accompanied by a fever and severe pain in many parts of the body. It typically lasted three or four days, after which most patients tended to recover rapidly from the disease.[172] However, occasionally, the influenza had the tendency to turn into either pneumonia or meningitis, each of which had the potential to be fatal.[173] However, such cases were few and far between.

In Springfield, for instance, only 53 of the first 1200 reported cases in the region were known to have been fatal, approximately 4.42% of all cases up to that time.[174] Next, the bulletin gave some of the tell-tale signs for recognizing a person who had contracted the disease; one of which was the exhibition of an abnormally high fever by the patient, which could reach temperatures as high as 104°F.[175]

One of the things which made this strain of influenza and this epidemic particularly perplexing for medical professionals at this time, was that unlike diseases such as smallpox or scarlet fever, which typically guarded a person from catching the disease again if he or she had had it previously, with Spanish Influenza, the case was the opposite. Just because a person had contracted influenza once before did not mean he or she was immune to catching a different or modified strain of the same disease at some later date.[176] Two such individuals who had such a misfortune were King Alfonso XIII and Lawrence Reed. King Alfonso XIII who was the ruler of Spain at the time, was one of the first Spaniards to contract the disease in the spring of 1918.[177] Lawrence, who according to Gladys's letters,[178] [179] appears to have had two mild cases of the influenza, one in the Fall of 1918 and the other in the Spring of 1919, both of which were presumably contracted from one of his co-workers at Bryant. In order to protect those people who were living under the same roof as someone who had contracted the virus, Surgeon General Blue provided numerous suggestions which people could take advantage of in order to protect themselves and others from contracting the disease. Among Blue's suggestions were: not allowing anyone to sleep in the same room as one with the disease and the wearing of an apron, a mask or some other article by the one who was tending to the patient in order to protect the attendant from either inhaling the germs or getting them on their regular clothes.[180] Blue further advised those who were still healthy to avoid having any direct contact with those who had contracted the disease by avoiding crowds, eating well, and having a proper balance of work, play and rest.[181] When a crowd situation was unavoidable, Blue advised people not breathe in the direction of air exhaled by another person so as to always inhale fresh air from their surroundings.[182]

The one suggestion of Blue's which many people did not hold to, but proved to be very beneficial when it came to combating the disease especially in case of the Reeds, was having regular exposure to fresh air. According to Blue, one of the best remedies for combating the flu virus was exposure to fresh or pure air.[183] Some families, like the Reeds, accomplished this multiple ways, including keeping their windows open as often as they as could.[184]

Lawrence was also able to get adequate exposure to fresh air each day by walking to and from work on a regular basis and by spending many evenings tending to the local war garden. However, he did take a few days off from work; at which time the Reed family took a vacation in order to get away for a few days. Gladys believed the time spent away from Springfield and the shop were the main contributors to Lawrence's rather speedy recovery from this first case of influenza.[185] However, upon returning from their short vacation to Feeding Hills and Gladys's sister, Edna; they learned that their neighbors, the Templetons, had both contracted the disease. Therefore, the Reeds did as much as they could to keep away from them while they were ill.[186] The bulletin closed with a little rhyme, "Cover up each cough and sneeze, if you don't you'll spread disease,"[187] which was designed to remind people to do as much as they could to keep the virus from spreading by keeping their germs to themselves.

In response to the flu epidemic, Springfield's Board of Health convened a meeting on September 28th, solely for the purpose of discussing what sort of measures they and the townspeople could take to: one, care for those who had already become stricken with the disease and two, keep the spread of the virus in the town under control and to a minimum.[188] At this meeting, which was led by the local health officer, Dr. B.A. Chapman, the Board of Health decided to order the shutdown of many public facilities until further notice, including schools, churches and the local theater, known as the Ideal Theater.[189] Five days later, on October 3rd, the local phone company put out a request for people to limit their phone conversions as much as possible, due to the fact the epidemic had left the phone company with only a limited number of healthy operators and as such, were having a tough time keeping up with the regular volume of phone calls made to and from Springfield.[190] On October 5th, Dr. Chapman's report told of 692 known influenza cases in the region, 31 of which had turned into pneumonia, of which 9 had proven to be fatal. On the same day and in light of the high volume of flu cases, an emergency hospital was set up with the assistance of the Red Cross, with the specific purpose of housing and treating those who had contracted the influenza virus. The hospital was established in the former residence of Walter White at 200 Clinton Street, Springfield, and was run by Mrs. Dan R. Barney with a team of ten doctors, nurses, teachers and a housekeeper from Springfield and the surrounding towns such as Ludlow, Vermont.[191]

When cases of Spanish Influenza began to appear in the United States in the summer of 1918, the Public Health Service needed to develop a way of determining the number of flu cases in a given area; while also classifying each case in terms of its severity. By doing this, the Public Health Service would be able determine the amounts of aid and assistance which were needed in order to curb the spread of the disease, while helping those who had already contracted it. During the late summer and fall of 1918, Public Health Statistician Edgar Sydenstricker, began to conduct field studies in a couple test sites around the country in order to get a sense of just how significantly the flu epidemic was impacting the lives of American citizens. Using Baltimore, Maryland as his main test location, Sydenstricker developed a classification system which he used to categorize each case of Spanish Influenza by its severity. When it came to classifying the types of flu cases, Sydenstricker divided them into three categories: Influenza, Pneumonia and Doubtful.[192]

Cases classified as "Influenza" were cases which confined a person to bed for more than three days, but didn't necessarily turn fatal; as opposed to those cases which got classified as "Pneumonia" which were those cases of flu which morphed into pneumonia and more often than not, proved to be fatal in the end. What made a case classified as "Doubtful" different from one classified as "Influenza" was the infected person would make a full recovery in only one or two days which was faster than the "normal" recovery period for influenza which was three days.[193] There were some medical experts who believed these more mild cases of influenza were in fact just bad colds and not flu at all. Given Lawrence Reed's very rapid recoveries from the flu, two days in each case, he may have been one whose bouts with influenza may have in reality just been a pair of bad colds.

Chapter 11
Soldiers' Letters:
A Healthy Distraction

Even though newspapers, like the *Springfield Reporter*, were filled with depressing stories about the flu epidemic, many of which were tributes and remembrances for the most recent victims of the disease, the success of the Allied Forces in France as they continued to push the Germans back towards Berlin provided many Americans with a happy, healthy distraction and alternative to the somber passages regarding influenza. While many of the pieces regarding the war were in the form of soldiers' letters and, due to the long distance which they had to travel, often appeared in the newspapers a month or more after they'd been initially written, they still provided the American people back home with a glimpse of what the soldiers' lives were like on the battlefront as well as an opportunity to read first-hand accounts of what was going on overseas.

One such letter was written by James L. McFadden to his grandfather on Independence Day 1918 and was subsequently published in the *Springfield Reporter* about a month later in its August 8th issue. McFadden, who was the captain of U.S. Submarine Chaser 83, tells his grandfather about what life was like on board one of these small patrol vessels.[194] According to McFadden, one of the toughest things for the men aboard a submarine chaser to get used to was the numerous times each day the submarine chasers would lose sight of either each other or the ship they were guarding. These momentary lapses of vision were caused by huge ocean currents which were typically taller than the chasers themselves. McFadden referred to these currents as "great walls of water."[195] USS SC-83 was one of 441 SC-1 Class submarine chasers built by the United States between 1917 and 1919. Each of these boats was 110 feet long, displaced 85 tons, had a top speed of 18 knots and was made primarily of wood. It was the job of a submarine chaser to do exactly what its name suggests which was to chase away and if necessary attack the German submarines, known as U-Boats, which were a constant threat to the larger ships of the United States Navy, such as battleships and destroyers.

In the following week's issue of the *Springfield Reporter*, a letter written by Sergeant Edward Bushour, tells the story of how the 103rd Machine Gun Battalion was successful in flushing out an encampment of German soldiers who had fled their post at the sight of the American bayonets.[196] Other letters, such as the one written by Lieutenant Jason B. Hart on July 5, 1918 and published the following August 22nd, provided an insight not just into the lives of the soldiers in the field of battle, but also into what their lives were like when they weren't actually confronted by enemy troops. Aside from a description of the old French town of Besanor, which was where Lieutenant Hart's unit was stationed in July 1918, Lieutenant Hart's letter talks about what the soldiers did to fill some of their free time in between battles. According to Lieutenant Hart, one of the most popular forms of entertainment amongst the soldiers was inter-squad baseball games which would pit teams from two different regiments against each other. If nothing else, these games provided all the soldiers with a way get out their competitive juices without having to be on the front lines fighting Germans. At the same time, such games also gave the soldiers, both as players and as spectators, a friendly reminder of home in the middle of a distant land.[197]

As the summer of 1918 began to wind down and turn to fall, so did the fortune of the Germans. The letters home from soldiers which began to cover the pages of the *Springfield Reporter* began to tell of increased success by the Allied Armies against their German adversaries. In separate letters to his mother, father and sister, George Wilder tells of how he and his fellow soldiers got their first opportunity to leave the trenches to attack the German Lines and in the process killed his first German. At the same time, Wilder also included some of the drawbacks of trench warfare in his letters. For instance, water was at premium and things such as milk were almost completely unavailable to the soldiers unless they were able to procure some in one of the nearby French villages. Like many of his fellow soldiers, Wilder also found the time to get his hands on some German souvenirs which he sent back to his family. Among the souvenirs Wilder obtained were: a cigarette box which he sent to his father and a German Boche knife which he sent to his sister.[198] Another Springfield resident, Porter T. Babcock had a slightly different way of giving the people back home a glimpse into the life of a soldier on the front lines. As a member of the 42nd or "Rainbow" Division, Babcock was among the first Americans to arrive and see action in France. In order to give his friends and family back home a very vivid picture of what he and his fellow soldiers went through in France, Babcock sent copies of two orders back home which commend his division for their bravery and performance in the field in the trenches of Lorraine and Champagne, France during the summer of 1918. His parents in turn, submitted these copies of the orders to the *Springfield Reporter* which were then published in the newspaper's October 10, 1918 issue.

Even though, the Influenza Epidemic was taking a toll on both the Red Cross and the citizens at large, they both still had the war on their minds and the soldiers' best interests at heart. A fourth Liberty Loan campaign was started in the New England area in late September 1918,[199] while the Red Cross was making arrangements for the families to send Christmas parcels to their friends and loved ones overseas.[200] The obvious goal of these holiday packages was it was a way to help boost the morale of soldiers, who at the time still didn't know that the war would be over long before the Christmas holiday came around that year. The only requests which the Red Cross made when it came to the Christmas packages was for the families to only use the 3x4x9 inch boxes which they provided and to not include any items in the packages which the Post Office considered contraband.[201] Not long after defeating the Germans at St. Mihiel on September 15th, the Allied Troops, led by General John Pershing and the American Expeditionary Force (AEF), commenced what would prove to be the final major offensive of the Great War, known as the Meuse-Argonne Offensive. As the Allies' drive through the Argonne Forest continued to push the German Troops further and further back towards Berlin, it began to become very clear, both on the front lines and back on the homefront, of how the Allies had every intention of trying to end the war before the year turned over to 1919. This hope must have seemed more and more like a possible reality as each day passed; especially as the Allies began to run off numerous victories over their German adversaries in fairly rapid succession at places such as Somme-Py (Sept. 26th), Saint-Thierry (Sept. 30th), Grand-Pre (Oct. 16th) and Montfaucon (Oct. 17th).

Perhaps seeing the handwriting on the wall after the first couple of defeats at Somme-Py and Saint-Thierry, the four main countries which made up the Central Powers, starting with Bulgaria and Austria-Hungary reached out to President Wilson in hopes of opening up armistice and peace negotiations which would put an end to the war. These initial two requests came in during the last days of September, with the leader of the Central Powers, Germany, sending a similar telegram on October 6th. While agreements with Bulgaria and Austria-Hungary were made rather expeditiously, Wilson decided on October 14th not to open such negotiations with the Germans at that time. The reasons for this were two fold. First, both Austria-Hungary and Bulgaria were very open to accepting all of President Wilson's Fourteen Points, a series of principles for world peace, which Wilson laid out in a speech to Congress the previous January 8th. The Allies would use the concepts in the Fourteen Points as a basis when it came to negotiating the armistices and peace agreements with each of the Central Powers. Secondly, both Austria-Hungary and Bulgaria reached out to all the Allied nations with regards to their armistices, while Germany chose to only contact the United States. As such, Wilson did not feel comfortable negotiating such a treaty without the involvement of the other Allied powers and so for the Germans, the war kept going. The fighting would persist until November 7th when American and French Troops captured the main railroad station in Sedan, France, which completely severed the supply lines which the Germans had been relying on to keep their forces reinforced and well armed. Realizing that they couldn't fight on much longer without the ability to resupply and bring in additional soldiers, the Germans and Allied nations agreed to an armistice on November 11, 1918, four days after the fighting had ceased. Also known as the Armistice of Compiegne in honor of the French city within which it was signed, this treaty and the war it concluded are celebrated each year on November 11th, a day which came to be known as "Armistice Day"; until it was renamed "Veterans Day" in 1954.

Back on the homefront, the last couple weeks of October also proved to be a very fortuitous time for the American people. Along with reading about the successful exploits of their friends and family in uniform in Allied victories, such as the one at Saint Mihiel, many Springfield residents also began to believe that the negative impact of the flu epidemic had reached its peak and was starting to improve. Many saw this as an indication of how life around town could begin to settle down and return to normal. Men began returning to the shops, while the schools and other local businesses started reopening their doors during the first week of November. These new positive feelings got reinforced when it was determined that the emergency hospital on Clinton Street could close down on October 26th. During its three weeks of operation, the makeshift hospital, a place which Gladys referred to as the "Big Yellow House,"[202] treated and cared for 41 patients with Spanish Influenza, including 18 of the 65 residents whose cases in the end proved to be fatal. The residents of Springfield further showed their appreciation for those who had worked tirelessly to care for their affected friends and family members, by filling the October 24, 1918 issue of the *Springfield Reporter* with a wide variety of thank-you notes and other similar expressions.

As far as Springfield was concerned, the epidemic was officially over when the headline in the *Springfield Reporter* said it was in its October 31, 1918 issue. The two other things which the paper mentioned as signs of the epidemic being over, at least locally, were the closure of the Emergency Hospital on Clinton Street, as well as the report of no new cases of the disease having been discovered the previous week. In the end, a conservative estimate of 300,000 to 350,000 Americans perished as a result of the Flu Epidemic or about 3 to 4 per every 1000 cases nationwide.[203] The most severely impacted areas were those which were more densely populated or of greater population overall. Population density and totals also had an impact on how long it took the virus to leave an area. Usually the greater the population of an area was, the longer the disease was likely to remain in said area.[204] Perhaps the most interesting statistic with regards to the flu's impact resulted from an immunity which school children seemed to have to the virus morphing into pneumonia. In many parts of the country, school children and infants had both some the highest rates of cases overall, as well as some of the lowest rates when it came to fatal cases, such as those which became pneumonia.[205] However, even though the schools were permitted to reopen on the 4th of November, other public gatherings were still prohibited from taking place. All of this would get completely disregarded when news of the Great War's conclusion became known.

Three days after the schools and a few other buildings were allowed to reopen (November 4th), the streets of Springfield were filled with hundreds of citizens, whose shouts of joy were complemented and backed up by church bells and shop whistles. Earlier in the day (November 7th), word had come from France about the capturing of the railroad station in Sedan by American and French forces; a maneuver which would be the last major exchange of bullets between the Allies and the Central Powers in the Great War, with the two sides beginning to engage in armistice talks that very evening. However, according to General Pershing, none of the Allies' success in northern France would have been possible without the "unrivaled fortitude" and "spirit of determination" in the face of continuous inclement weather and lack of advantageous fighting positions throughout the final weeks of battle.[206]

Even with the German Armies in a full retreat in late October 1918, General Pershing and his fellow commanders knew that if the Allies wanted to bring a swift end to the fighting and not risk continuing the war into the following year or later, the Allies would have to cut off at least one of the Germans' two main supply and evacuation routes through northern France and

Belgium; before the German troops could make it through the Ardennes and back to Germany. If the Germans were able to pull off a successful retreat and get their remaining forces back to Germany without being cut off by the Allies, there would be nothing to prevent them from reorganizing and mounting a counterattack in the near future. At this time, due to its very mountainous terrain, there were only two east-west railway passages through the Ardennes in northern France – one in the north which passed through Liege, Belgium and a second one further south which passed through Sedan. These two routes were also the two main avenues which the Germans used to keep their forces both reinforced and well supplied with things such as food and ammunition. The Germans would also use these two railways to evacuate their forces from the region, should the need to do so ever arise. As such, the loss of either route would more than likely be a crippling blow to the German forces in Northern France, especially if the larger of the two routes, the one which passed through Sedan, fell into the hands of the Allies. With that in mind, General Pershing chose to focus his attack on the railroad station at Sedan, which was the most strategic point on the stretch of track known as the Carignan–Mezieres Railroad, a four-track stretch which almost two thirds of the German Army relied upon for reinforcements, supplies and escape.[207] Such a loss would most likely make Germany's ability to extend the war into the following year impractical, if not impossible.

On November 1, 1918, General Pershing and Marshal Foch had their respective armies lined up from the Meuse River to Bois de Bourgogne to Grand-Pre and were poised to begin the third and final phase of the Meuse-Argonne Offensive; which, if successful, would sever the critical Carignan–Mezieres Railroad at Sedan and with any luck bring a swift end to the Great War. If everything went according to plan, the American First Army would charge up from the south, with the hopes of breaking the German defensive positions between Verdun and Sedan, while the French Fourth Army would attack from the west of the Argonne Forest and capture Mezieres, before turning southeast and marching towards Sedan where they would have the honor of entering the city first ahead of the Americans.[208] Over the next few days and often preceded by a barrage of artillery fire to soften the German lines, the soldiers of the American First and the French Fourth Armies charged through and around the Argonne Forest towards Sedan, capturing and driving the Germans out of the towns of Aincreville, Andrevanne, Barricourt and Buzcany, among others.[209]

By November 5th, the American heavy artillery was in position to begin shelling the Carignan–Mezieres Railroad, including some key junction spots at Longuyon and Conflans; after having all but driven the German Army out of their wooded strongholds in the Argonne Forest. It would take just another two days for all three corps of the American First Army to establish strong fighting positons on the Meuse Heights, across the river from Sedan, while the men of the French Fourth Army were given the honor of being the first Allied troops to enter the city. At this time, having now had their main line of supplies and communications severed, the Germans realized that "nothing but a cessation of hostilities could save their armies from complete disaster"[210] and annihilation. As such, the Germans promptly appealed to the Allies for an immediate beginning of negotiations for an armistice along with an immediate ceasefire on the evening of November 6th, not long after the American First Army began establishing their positions on the heights overlooking Sedan. It was this immediate end of hostilities and subsequent armistice which prompted thousands of Americans all across the country to partake in a variety of day-long celebrations on November 7th and 11th respectively.

If there was one thing which separated November of 1918 from other Novembers, it was the plethora of celebrations and festivities which occurred throughout the month on a nationwide scale. After spending two of the previous five days celebrating their country's success in leading the Allies to victory in the Great War, many Americans started to turn their attention towards preparing for the next big national holiday, which was Thanksgiving. Set to take place on November 28th, this Thanksgiving held a special significance for many Americans, whose previous eighteen months were full of stress and heartache as they watched their friends and loved ones go off to war; not knowing if they would ever see them again. As such, the Armistice with Germany could not have come at a more appropriate time of year, as many Americans echoed the message of President Wilson, who in his yearly Thanksgiving Proclamation (#1496) asked the country to take a couple extra minutes on that day to remember and honor the men and women who had sacrificed so much both at home and overseas to defend their freedoms, liberties and way of life.

Chapter 12

Thanksgiving 1918: A Soldier's Feast

Even though the capture of Sedan and the subsequent signing of the Armistice brought an end to the Great War, many American soldiers would still find themselves in France for at least another month or more; while the Allies determined how many men and supplies would be needed to oversee the peaceful transition and rebuilding of Germany following the abdication of Kaiser Wilhelm. As a result, many of these same soldiers ended up celebrating Thanksgiving in 1918 in places other than their own homes. However, when looking at some of the delicacies which these soldiers partook in, one could conclude that the troops overseas enjoyed far more extravagant Thanksgiving meals than any of their friends and families could have ever imagined!

One commonality among the Thanksgiving feasts, which American service personnel all over the world enjoyed in 1918, was each one had numerous courses with each course having multiple options of delicacies to be partaken in. On the homefront, for instance, the soldiers and sailors stationed at places like Fort Mifflin (Philadelphia, PA), Camp Wadsworth (Spartanburg, SC), Camp Funston (Fort Riley, KS), Camp Hancock (Augusta, GA), Camp Sheridan (Montgomery, AL) and the Newport (RI) Naval Torpedo Station all enjoyed some version of turkey for their main course, with baked spiced ham and larded tenderloin of beef also being found on the tables at Newport and Camp Hancock respectively. In each case, the turkeys these men enjoyed were roasted and stuffed with a mayonnaise, oyster or sage stuffing, which was then served as a side dish with the turkey. Other common side dishes included some form of cranberry sauce; giblet gravy, mashed potatoes and yams or sweet potatoes, which usually were candied. However, each of these Thanksgiving tables also had at least one side dish which was more unique to the table with which it was found on. For example, the men stationed at Fort Mifflin enjoyed celery and creamed corn; while cauliflower and a Delmonico salad, which was a lettuce based salad with cheese, eggs, tomatoes and bacon, were enjoyed by those stationed at the Naval Torpedo Station in Newport, Rhode Island. The Delmonico salad was actually a take on the house salad which was served at the famous Delmonico's Restaurant in New York City, having been introduced by its head chef, Alessandro Filippini, about a half century earlier.[211] The only other side dish which was not found on all of the aforementioned Thanksgiving tables, was bread and butter, which the men stationed at Camp Wadsworth had the pleasure of enjoying.

However, since all of these Thanksgiving tables featured five course meals, there was one course which needed to be enjoyed before the entrees and side dishes were brought out, which was known as the starter course or the hors d'oeuvres. Most of the foods which were enjoyed during this course were what today we might call "finger foods". The majority of the starters enjoyed by soldiers, who were stateside, fell into the vegetable category and included olives, pickles, celery, lettuce, onions, radishes and yams. The other popular starter at these meals was soup, specifically oyster and cream of celery each of which was accompanied by some type of cracker. Mixed nuts and fruits, such as apples, bananas, raisins and oranges were also commonplace throughout the evening. After everyone had had their fill of starters, entrée and sides, the next course to hit the table was dessert, which most commonly was pie and more specifically pumpkin pie. However, apple, mince and squash pies could each be found on at least one Thanksgiving table in 1918. Aside from pie, the soldiers also enjoyed candy, chocolate cake, fruit cake, jelly roll, ice cream, Allied plum pudding and Hancock bread, when it came time for dessert. All this food got washed down with coffee, cider or root beer and was commonly capped off with an after dinner cigar or a cigarette or two. While the Thanksgiving meals enjoyed by the soldiers, who had already returned home, appear to have been quite lavish and sophisticated, they didn't compare to the similar meals which the soldiers who were still overseas enjoyed that same evening.

The first two Thanksgiving meals which were enjoyed by the soldiers overseas to consider were those which took place aboard the USS Georgia (BB-15) and the USS Agamemnon. The USS Georgia was the third of five Virginia class battleships built by the United States Navy between 1902 and 1907. Launched in 1904, she was one of sixteen American battleships which circumnavigated the globe as part of the Great White Fleet; which had the intent of showcasing the strength and might of the U.S. Navy to the world during a time of peace. When the United States declared war on Germany on April 6, 1917, the Georgia was one of several ships who were recommissioned and assigned to the Atlantic Fleet to be a training vessel for a variety of tactical and gunnery exercises.[212] In September 1918, after having been a training vessel for the first sixteen months of the United States' involvement in the Great War, the Georgia was reassigned to the Cruiser Force Atlantic; which was tasked with escorting Allied convoys to the middle of the Atlantic Ocean, where a different group of ships would take over escorting the convoys from there until they reached their destinations in England.[213] After the Great War ended, the Georgia was repurposed to be a transport ship and made five voyages to and from France; during which time, she managed to bring over 6,000 soldiers home. As a result of these new, post-war duties, the men and crew of the Georgia found themselves enjoying their 1918 Thanksgiving meal aboard ship in the middle of the North Atlantic as opposed to being either home on dry land or docked in a friendly harbor. A meal which one might think may have been very simplistic having probably taken place out at sea could actually be far better described as rather "lavish" as opposed to "simple", especially given some of the delicacies the men of the Georgia had the privilege of enjoying for their Thanksgiving meal on the evening of November 28, 1918. Along with bread and butter, the men of the Georgia enjoyed Consommé, a hot French soup which is a clear broth made by boiling meat and/

or vegetables to extract their nutritious aspects and is then further clarified by straining it and then adding egg whites to it to absorb the remaining excess fat.[214] For the main course, the men had a choice of either roast turkey or spiced ham, which were served with sides such as giblet gravy, oyster dressing (stuffing), cranberry sauce, mashed potatoes, turnips and sugar corn. Finally for dessert, the men had a choice of ice cream, pound cake or pumpkin pie; all of which got chased down by coffee, cigars and cigarettes.

The only similarities the USS Georgia had with the USS Agamemnon is they were both built at about the same time (1904 and 1902) and they both played a role in the Allied war effort; during and after the Great War. However, the beginnings of each ship's life, as well as its indoctrination to service to the United States, couldn't be more different. On one hand, the USS Georgia was a U.S. Government commissioned pre-dreadnought battleship from the day its hull was first laid down in 1901; while the USS Agamemnon actually began life in the Shipyard of AG Vulcan in Stettin, Germany as the SS Kaiser Wilhelm II, a nearly 20,000 ton German, high speed, high class, trans-Atlantic passenger ocean liner which made regular trips between Germany and New York in the decade leading up to the Great War (1904-1914). She even set a trans-Atlantic speed record in 1904. With war between Germany and Great Britain being declared on August 4, 1914, the Kaiser Wilhelm II's career as a commercial ocean liner came to an end two days later when it arrived in New York and became interned there for the next 32 months. It was then taken over by the U.S. Government on April 6, 1917, the day the United States entered the Great War. Over the next few months, the Kaiser Wilhelm II would go through an extensive overhaul before being recommissioned the following August as an American troop transport named the USS Kaiser Wilhelm II, a name which was changed to the USS Agamemnon on September 1, 1917. The Agamemnon would then spend the remainder of the war and the months immediately after ferrying American soldiers to and from France; without fail and with very little loss of life, even despite an influenza outbreak on the ship in the fall of 1918.

Thanksgiving of 1918 found the Agamemnon undergoing voyage repairs; which meant even though the ship was out at sea, it was probably hanging close to its home base in Hoboken, New Jersey while repair crews were brought to and from the ship on a daily basis to conduct the repairs. Like the Georgia, the feast the men aboard the Agamemnon enjoyed for Thanksgiving on November 28, 1918, was "lavish" to say the least. For starters the men partook in cream of asparagus soup and a combination salad, which contained meat or chicken as well as vegetables along with oyster cocktails. Like the Georgia, there were two choices for the main course: roasted turkey and sugared hams. These were accompanied by side dishes of oyster dressing (stuffing), cranberry sauce, sugar corn, celery, mashed potatoes, candied sweet potatoes, sweet pickles and queen olives. The drink of choice was coffee and more specifically black coffee; however, unlike many Thanksgiving dinners that year; there were no pies when it came time to have dessert. Instead the men enjoyed a selection of fruits, nuts and cakes, as well as ice cream and candy. While the only available ice cream flavor was most likely vanilla, the types of candy the soldiers might have enjoyed included assorted chocolates, stick candy, lemon drops,[215] chewing gum,[216] and peanut chews.[217] In fact, starting in the summer of 1918, the popularity and demand for chewing gum constantly grew at a steady rate as many of the soldiers found it to be a suitable replacement for water on long marches and, in a few instances, a healthier replacement for chewing tobacco.[218] As for the peanut chews, which were made by Goldenberg's in Philadelphia, PA, the U.S. Military used them as a rations bar and became very popular with the soldiers due to their unique dark chocolate taste as well as their high protein and high energy properties.[219] Lastly, like many of the other Thanksgiving meals that year, many of the soldiers also partook in after dinner cigars and cigarettes with their coffee and dessert. For some of the soldiers though, their Thanksgiving meals in 1918 were actually somewhat atypical as compared to the more traditional meals enjoyed by their families and friends back on the homefront. For those soldiers who were still stationed in France after Armistice Day, the Thanksgiving meals they enjoyed in 1918 were very much influenced and highlighted by aspects of the French cuisine, on both a local and national level.

The two Thanksgiving menus which hail from France are those which detail what was on the table for the men stationed at the 2nd Aviation Instruction Center in Tours and for the men of the 94th Aero Squadron; whose exact location at this time is not detailed as they attempted to keep their exact whereabouts hidden from the Germans. In cases such as that of the 94th, the only way their whereabouts got openly designated was as "Somewhere in France". However, according to service records, one will see that the 94th was stationed at the Rembercourt (France) Aerodrome from August 30th to December 8th, 1918 and as such it was probably there the men of the 94th enjoyed their Thanksgiving meal before being transferred to Trier in Germany a couple weeks later.

One of the most noticeable differences between the Thanksgiving meals enjoyed by the soldiers in France as opposed to those in other places is how the more traditional main dish of turkey was not always necessarily the highlighted entrée or even on the menu at all. In Tours for instance, while there was roasted turkey with a chestnut dressing on the menu, the dish which commanded the top line of the main course part of the Tours menu was boiled whitefish with Chateau-Thierry sauce. Most likely, this dish was made by boiling a white-fleshed fish such as trout, mullet, pike, perch, bream or catfish; which was then served with a sauce made with the local Chateau Thierry wine, Champagne Pannier NV, a sparkling wine made from three varieties of grapes which give it the finesse of a Chardonnay, the structure of a Pinot Noir and the delicateness of a Pinot Meunier.[220] On the other hand, the men at Rembercourt only had one choice for a main dish that evening and it wasn't turkey, but rather roast pork with sauce. Aside from one or two things, such as fruit or fruit salad and some type of cake, the menus from Rembercourt and Tours differed in just about every way, with each one having both French inspired elements as well as the more traditional American elements. For side dishes, while the men in Tours partook in cranberry sauce and a crab salad, the men of the 94th enjoyed the more traditional mashed potatoes and other root vegetables found on the tables back on the homefront. For dessert, the two menus featured an assortment of cakes, candy, pies, puddings and tarts. Finally, in celebration of the

Armistice, the drink which came to be known as "Armistice Punch" was invented. It was made by dissolving 1.5 cups of sugar in one cup of water, which was then added to a cup of orange juice and a half cup of lemon juice. This entire mixture was then strained over ice into a punch bowl. A pint each of ginger ale and Lithia were then added right before the drink was to be served and, lastly, it was garnished with thin slices of orange and some preserved cherries.[221]

The last Thanksgiving menu which bears some attention, is one which considering the number of choices it had as well as the types of food it had on it, is in a class all its own. Since the Philippines were a territory of the United States during the first half of the 20th century, the United States military constantly maintained a presence in and around Southeast Asia during that time. As a result, it was the men of the USS Wilmington, among others, who found themselves in this area of the world during the Great War, charged with patrolling the waters and coastlines of the U.S.-held territories in the region; just in case the Germans attempted to open up another front during the war in hopes of weakening the Allied forces by forcing them to spread out further across the globe than they had adequate manpower to cover. Since most of the territory patrolled by the USS Wilmington at this time was the route in between Shanghai, China and Manila Bay, Philippines, it makes sense that the men of the USS Wilmington found themselves anchored in the harbor of Manila Bay on Thanksgiving 1918.

If there is one word which can be used to characterize the menu given to the men of the USS Wilmington on November 28, 1918, it is "choices". Each of the initial four courses on this menu had at least four choices under them. Another phrase which can be used to describe the Thanksgiving meal enjoyed by the men of the USS Wilmington is "soup to nuts", which is a late 19th century expression, meaning the entire or all of something. In this case, the "soup" refers to one of the first courses in a formal multi-course meal, while the "nuts" refers to one of the final courses enjoyed during a formal multi-course meal. The 12-course meal, which the men of the USS Wilmington enjoyed began with an oyster cocktail, a very traditional starter to a formal meal at that time. This cocktail however, was not an hors d'oeuvre in the way hors d'oeuvres are thought of today. A formal meal in the early 20th century would actually have a cocktail starter, with an hors d'oeuvres course coming later on. For the second course, which was known as the "potage" or "soup" course, the men were served cream of tomato soup, which was then followed by the hors d'oeuvres course. For this third course, the men sampled a variety of relishes, such as chow chow, which was a sweet pickled relish made with vegetables such as cabbage, onions and peppers;[222] as well as an assortment of vegetable dishes which included ripe stuffed olives, celery, sliced tomatoes, green onions and wilted lettuce. After the initial three courses, all of which contained foods which were light in nature, the next four courses in order were all main dishes namely the fish or "poisson" (4), the entrée (5), the roast or "roti" (6) and the cold meats or "releves" (7). The menu for these courses included fried halibut with tartar sauce (Fish), stuffed bell peppers with tomato sauce (Entrée), suckling pig or young goose (Roast) and sliced ham or ox tongue with cream cheese (Cold Meats). There were also side dishes of chestnut dressing for the pork and spiced gravy for the goose as well as cranberry sauce. While not a course in the purest sense, the eighth course was made up of more vegetable side dishes including cream(ed) asparagus tips and mashed potatoes as well as French peas, sliced beets and sweet corn. The next three courses were different things one could enjoy for dessert, assuming anybody had the room to cram anymore food into their already very stuffed bellies that night. Desserts included an assortment of pies, puddings and cakes (9) along with strawberry ice cream (10) and a variety of fruits, nuts and candy (11). The final part of this lavish 12-course meal was a cup of black coffee known as "café noir" and after dinner cigars or cigarettes. There was also lemonade and lemon(e)d iced tea served throughout the evening.

With the signing of the Armistice, the Cruiser and Transport Force, the branch of U.S. Navy responsible for getting the troops and the necessary supplies over to France during the war, immediately shifted its focus to getting the men back home to their families and friends; some of whom hadn't seen each other in over a year. With the end of all submarine warfare and the surrender of the entire U-Boat force, as per the 22nd stipulation of the Terms of the Armistice, the men on the transport ships no longer had to worry about being attacked by German submarines while making the long voyage across the Atlantic Ocean.[223] However, even though the soldiers began to return home to their friends and families not long after the signing of the Armistice, the men and women overseas still had a major job ahead of them as the United States had the responsibility of overseeing and aiding Germany and France in their efforts to rebuild following the hostilities of the previous four years. At the same time, the work and effort by those on the homefront in support of the soldiers and nurses overseas also continued with the same eagerness, fortitude and high level of productivity.

The United States Military would maintain a rather significant occupation force in Europe until the conclusion of the negotiations at the Paris Peace Conference on May 7, 1919 in order to oversee the rebuilding of France and Germany following the Great War, while ensuring that no further hostilities erupted between the Central Powers and the Allied Nations. By the beginning of 1920, the number of soldiers who were still overseas in Germany and France totaled only a mere 15,000 men; with the last thousand departing the shores of Europe on January 24, 1923.[224]

Chapter 13

Armistice Signed, Wars Not Over

Just like their male compatriots, who wielded rifles and put their lives on the line to help defeat the Germans while coping with the brutalities of trench warfare, the women who volunteered to be Red Cross nurses worked tirelessly to care for the many wounds and ailments suffered by both soldiers and civilians as a result of the hostilities. Following the signing of the Armistice, many of these same nurses remained in Europe well into the following year in order to aid and assist the many victims of the Influenza Epidemic. As such the need to keep the soldiers and nurses well supplied with all the necessary munitions, clothes and medical supplies continued for several months after the war officially ended and the American people did not disappoint their countrymen overseas. In her letter   of December 15, 1918 to her sister Edna, Gladys tells how she, Mrs. Templeton and some of the other women in Springfield continued to knit stockings for the American Red Cross,[225] while presumably, the men, such as Lawrence continued to produce the necessary ammunition shells needed by the soldiers. Even though, the machine shops in Springfield were still producing munitions casings after the signing of the Armistice, the end of the hostilities meant that the need for such products had been greatly reduced; leading the Department of Defense to cancel many of the contracts it had with all the machine shops along the Black River and in Precision Valley. In turn, the loss of these contracts left Lawrence and many of the other men in the area to wonder how much longer they were going to have their jobs with the machine shops, some maintaining the belief that the drop in demand would eventually lead to one or more rounds of job cuts[226] in the upcoming months and years, depending on how long the United States chose to maintain a military presence in Europe.

Along with the people's continuous efforts to support the men and women who were still overseas as soldiers and nurses, the patriotic fervor which the war effort inspired continued to influence the lives of those on the homefront when it came to some of their day to day activities and decision making. For instance, even though the war had been over for over a week, Wilcomb's, a dry goods   store in Springfield, ran an advertisement in the *Springfield Reporter* encouraging people to celebrate a "Patriotic Christmas" this year because buying their patriotic products was a demonstration of the "true American spirit" and in support of Uncle Sam.[227] A similar, but more detailed advertisement was run in the *Springfield Reporter* by W.H. Wheeler and Son on December 12, 1918; and it included two extensive lists of gift ideas for the fast approaching Christmas holiday, one for boys and one for girls.[228] The gifts offered by Wheeler's Store were billed as being for people of all ages "from baby to Grandpa", while ranging in price from a dime to hundreds of dollars. Gifts for boys and men included cigars, pipes, bill folds, razors, cuff links and pocket knives; while those for girls and women included perfumes, recipe files, books, diaries, jewelry and magazine subscriptions.[229] There were also a few gifts which could be found on both lists such as Kodaks (cameras), fountain pens, phonographs and records, one of which was *"Just a Baby's Prayer at Twilight"*, which was the largest selling record of the fall of 1918 and a record which Wheeler's had only 25 copies remaining in their inventory when this advertisement was printed.[230] Along with this record, "Wheeler's Colyum" was a short column printed on the far left side of its advertisement and it included a handful of blurbs, each one promoting one specific item from the lists of gift suggestions. Along with *"Just a Baby's Prayer at Twilight"*, other gifts which got highlighted were leather goods for men and boys; and a Corona typewriter for women and girls.

Even though the war had come to an end, the *Springfield Reporter* continued to receive and print copies of the letters submitted to them by their readers, many of which continued to describe in vivid detail what was going on overseas throughout the fall and early winter. On December 19, 1918, the *Springfield Reporter* published the letter which John Russell Knights wrote to his mother and sisters on November 16, 1918, in which he details the festivities which took place in Tours, France when the news of the signing of the Armistice became known.[231] Based on what Knights writes in his letter, one thing which is clear is how the signing of the Armistice triggered these grand celebrations in cities, towns and villages all over each of the Allied Nations. Like Springfield, Tours became the scene of a grand, citywide celebration, one which included parades, marching bands, raucous festivities and people packed along the streets so tight, that barely anyone could move from where he or she stood. Also, when the news of the signing of Armistice began known, all the men of Tours promptly quit work for the day and went out to participate in the local festivities, very similar to what Lawrence and the other machinists did in Springfield. According to Knights, the Armistice celebration in Tours on November 11, 1918 was the first time the city's streetlights had been lit up in many months, perhaps as a sign of life beginning to return to normal in the area following the cessation of hostilities in the region. Knights also tells how throughout the entire celebration, much of the rest of the noise it created was drowned out by cheers of "Finis le guerre! Finis le guerre! Vive l'Amerique! Vive la France!"[232] which translates as "Finish the war! Finish the war! Long live America! Long live France!". The celebrations also gave many soldiers, such as Knights, an opportunity to do some sight-seeing and exploring, something many of them did not have the chance to do during the war itself.

Along with the end of the fighting in Europe, another thing which many Americans were able to celebrate as Christmas 1918 drew near were the constantly improving, weekly reports of new influenza cases in their local cities and regions. In fact, by Christmas Day, very little news about the epidemic or the influenza itself was heard in places like Springfield, Vermont – "Don't hear much about the 'flu' up here although the doctors claim there are still a few scattering cases. I saw by the paper that Fred Humaston and Andy Arnold's wife both died. I feel sorry for the eight children she left behind."[233] While the number of influenza cases in and around Springfield seemed to be dropping by the week, Gladys couldn't help but acknowledge the presence of the disease in the area at the time, given that the local newspaper, the *Springfield Reporter*, was still making note of new victims of the disease in its weekly "Springfield Locals" column. However, in her letter of December 22, 1918 to Edna, Gladys very quickly moves on to the much happier subject of what different people were sending them for Christmas that year and in this instance it was what a very dear friend and matchmaker sent Lawrence and Gladys's 9-month old daughter Evelyn. "Margaret sent her a Christmas present and it's the cutest thing you ever saw — a plate, cup and saucer, knife, fork and spoon made of aluminum. I have never seen any just like it but it's very pretty and best of all she can't break it when she's big enough to use it".[234] For her very first Christmas, Evelyn Reed received a childsized, aluminum place setting from Margaret Brown, the woman who was responsible for getting Lawrence and Gladys to tie the knot, by independently suggesting to each of them that one would be an ideal spouse for the other. Given, how busy and active Evelyn was from a very early age, Gladys was probably very thankful that the set was made out of a seemingly unbreakable material such as aluminum as opposed to a more fragile material like china or porcelain. The aluminum set was the first of many gifts which neighbors, friends and family would shower upon the Reed's daughter for her very first Christmas and managed to do so without giving the Reeds any more gifts than they had received for any Christmas prior. Aside from the aluminum place setting from Margaret, Evelyn got baby pins from Gladys's good friend and classmate, Carrie Merchant; a silver cup with a gold lining from Edna and Ray Robinson; a white bonnet and mittens from Lawrence's parents; a blue and white rattle from Blanche; a little gold ring from their neighbor, Mrs. Templeton; and five dollars from Gladys and Edna's brother, Howard Steere.[235] Even though much of the attention, presents wise, was directed towards the new member of the family; Lawrence and Gladys each received a handful of gifts as well. From Carrie, Gladys received a collar,[236] which was a type of snug fitting band or necklace worn either around one's neck or at the neckline of a garment,[237] particularly one which had a neckline which was lower than desired. From her in-laws, she received enough material with which to make two waists,[238] which were a type of bodice in the nineteenth and early twentieth centuries; while two of her colleagues from normal school, Blanche and Doris, gave her a light blue boudoir cap[239] and a pair of mittens with some handkerchiefs respectively.[240] Handkerchiefs seemed to be a fairly popular gift in the Reed household for Christmas 1918, as that is what Lawrence received from both Blanche and his parents, who also gave him a tie as well. There were also more Christmas cards than could be listed within the confines of a single letter.

Not much is known about how the Reeds spent New Year's and the month of January 1919 because there are no letters which are still in existence from which detail such events. The reason for the lack of letters could possibly be because the family was all gathered for some reason in either Springfield or Feeding Hills or because the letters were lost either by being inadvertently thrown away or by getting destroyed as a result of water damage from a flood in the Reed household in Enfield, Connecticut some years later. The majority of what is known about what the Reeds may have done during the holiday season and New Year's 1918-19, comes from things written in the *Springfield Reporter* about what was going on at the different churches in the area, including the Methodist church, of which they were members. The only thing which may have kept the Reeds from participating in the different holiday events at the Methodist church in Springfield would be if they chose to spend the holidays in Feeding Hills with Edna and the rest of the Steere side of the family. According to the *Springfield Reporter*, the Methodist church had a special program for all the Sunday school classes on Christmas Eve, during which each of the classes got a visit from Santa Claus and then proceeded to each give a presentation, which was either a song or a story acted out. Lastly, all of the Sunday school students received a special gift from Santa Claus while standing under the church's Christmas tree.[241]

One thing the holidays brought to some families in Springfield was some assurance of the safe return of their friends and loved ones who had been fighting in Europe. The local newspaper also continued to print the letters written by the soldiers, as their families provided them to be published. However, given the lengthy duration of the voyage across the Atlantic Ocean, many of these letters did not appear in the newspaper till at least four to six weeks after they were initially written and mailed. As such, some of the letters published in the December 26, 1918 edition of the *Springfield Reporter*, were actually originally written back in November between the day the war ended and the beginning of December. One such letter, written on December 6, 1918, tells of the life and routine of an American sailor, whose ship was in a major accident and, as a result, ended up spending the last eight months of the war in a dry dock in Great Britain before being allowed to sail back home in December. Roy G. Faxon was a sailor aboard the USS Old Colony, an American steamship which was on her way over to Great Britain to be transferred to the Royal Navy and then get refitted as a minelayer. The USS Old Colony began her final journey as an American ship on November 12, 1917 and about three and a half weeks later, was moored just outside Halifax (Nova Scotia) Harbor, awaiting repairs to one of her boilers. On the morning of December 6, 1917, the Old Colony was rocked by the Great Halifax Explosion. American sailors from the Old Colony and other ships, like Faxon immediately organized themselves into search parties and began scouring the blast site for survivors. The skipper of the Old Colony, Captain Harold Hines, also ordered his ship to be moved further into Halifax Harbor, where she would be utilized as a hospital ship for a team of American naval surgeons, among others, in the days and weeks to come. After having repairs completed and being discharged from her duty as a floating temporary hospital, the Old Colony departed Halifax on May 10, 1918[242] and a month later arrived in London, England, where she was turned over to the British Government. Faxon and the rest of the Old Colony's crew were taken to Queenstown, Ireland and from there were reassigned to other American ships in the region.

Fortunately for Faxon and a few of his shipmates, they were assigned to the USS Manley (DD-74),[243] which was undergoing repairs in a dry dock in Liverpool following an onboard explosion which obliterated her stern back on March 19th. The explosion was caused by some depth charges in the Manley's hull, which got set off when the ship collided with the HMS Montague, just as she was about to finish escorting a convoy of soldiers and supplies from the United States. Since the skipper of the Manley had given his entire crew, "leave to go where he liked"[244] until the time when the repairs were completed, Faxon and the others who had been transferred from the Old Colony were afforded the same luxury upon arriving in Liverpool. As such, outside of his efforts during the aftermath of the Great Halifax Explosion, Roy Faxon was able to wait out the war for the most part in secure settings, something which probably gave his family and friends much comfort and peace of mind heading into the 1918 holiday season.

In many ways, the letters which the soldiers wrote back home after the Armistice got signed was one of the most comforting things their families and friends had because it assured them that their loved ones had survived the war and would be home sometime in the coming months, even if it wasn't in time for the holidays. What the soldiers' letters told their loved ones was that there were a myriad of ways to keep out of trouble with no more bullets being fired. For some soldiers, like Private 1st Class (PFC) Merle S. Whitcomb, being overseas in France in what was now a time of peace, offered them an opportunity to do some all-expenses paid sightseeing of the French countryside and its culture, an opportunity they probably would not have gotten at some later time. Soldiers, like Whitcomb, took the opportunity to really absorb the French atmosphere and culture in cities such as Bourges,[245] as they awaited their chance to hop one of the dozens of ships which were transporting the soldiers back to the United States. Feeling very comfortable in his surroundings, Whitcomb, in his letter of December 2, 1918 to his parents, wished that they and   all his family could be with him in France to celebrate the holidays that year because he was certain that they would all enjoy it.[246] There also another group of soldiers, who were able to absorb some French culture by continuing to interact with the French people as part of the occupation army, which had the job of helping the French people rebuild following four brutal years of war. According to a blurb in the *Springfield Reporter*, a nice rapport developed between the American soldiers and the French children, when the soldiers showed no hesitation when it came to sharing their "chow" with their little French friends. Any fear, the French children may have had of the soldiers, very quickly turned to admiration and adoration.[247] Such news, probably brought comfort and joy to the hearts of the families and friends of the soldiers who were involved in this rebuilding effort – that even though the soldiers weren't back home in the United States, they were helping the French get their homes back in order and in some cases in time for the holidays.

Chapter 14

1919

Having survived the holidays and New Year's, the Reeds, like all the families back in Springfield, were also trying to get their lives back to normal, especially with the war and the demands it had had on their lives over the past couple years no longer being issues. One of the key indicators of this is the tone and subject matters found within the letters they wrote to each other and to other friends. Between December 23, 1918 and February 8, 1919, there are no known letters written amongst the Reed family. Even though the letters could be presumed lost, more than likely, this was a time when the family was together very frequently and as such, the act of writing letters to tell people whom they had just seen, things they had just told them in person, would have seemed a little redundant and as such these letters were just never written to begin with. As opposed to during the war, when the letters were full of comments about how the war was impacting her family's lives, in this next group of letters, Gladys talked primarily about much more personal matters and things going on in each individual's life. For example in her letter of February 9, 1919 to her sister, Edna, Gladys talked about the housework she did and the books she was reading; while mentioning Evelyn's overwhelming desire to be successful at anything she set out to do and the fact that Lawrence was spending the day chopping wood.[248] In some ways the letter sounded more like a journal entry or one side of a light phone conversation, however since it was the most convenient way for two people to stay in touch on a regular basis, maybe individuals like Gladys and Edna used it to keep each other informed as to what was going on in their respective corners of the Reed/Steere universe.

Another thing about the letters between Gladys and Edna is they really varied both in length and content – it just depended on how busy each one's week was and how much each was willing to write. In her letter of the following week,[249] Gladys tells her sister about having to go to the dentist to get medicine put on a tooth with an abscess, which was fine except that she had to also tote Evelyn with her because no babysitter could be found and Lawrence was still working at Bryant, just like he had been doing before the war. This didn't seem to be a problem for the dentist who was able to keep Evelyn amused the entire time with some empty glass medicine bottles, which fit exactly with Gladys's observation that Evelyn always liked to be busy and out and about when awake. According to Gladys, Evelyn was a "bad egg" because she was always getting dirty and had a penchant for wanting to crawl into the fireplace all the time. After talking about her trip to the dentist and Evelyn for a while, Gladys talked about the housework and sewing she had done, before telling Edna everything she had cooked during the past week, including a pork roast from her; before wrapping up with some of the extra good deeds Lawrence was doing on top of his regular work, including housesitting for their neighbors, the Templetons.

Even though the war had come to an end, both on the battlefield and for the most part in the halls of government, the American Expeditionary Force and Red Cross both continued to maintain presences in Europe to help the area rebuild after the war and aid the many displaced civilians who had lost everything as a result of the war's destruction. For instance, in Springfield, women like Gladys Reed and the other members of the Young Women's Mission Club, continued to aid and assist the Red Cross back on the homefront, by meeting several times after the war's official conclusion, to sew and make dresses and other garments for the many refugee children who were now in Europe,[250] particularly in the war-devastated areas of France, Italy and Poland. Organized by a Mrs. Howe,[251] this selfless devotion of time, energy and expertise, demonstrated that the American people were always looking to lend a helping hand to their fellow man, even if that individual was overseas somewhere in a foreign country. At the same time though, every American welcomed each day when the number of soldiers and Red Cross personnel overseas dwindled, whether it be by one, a few or many.

March 1919 would prove to be a bit of a devilish month for the town of Springfield, Vermont. On the plus side, more soldiers from the area began to return home, including Frank Templeton, who came home from France with a plethora of souvenirs from the front lines, which he was more than willing to show off to whoever wanted to see them. However, he also managed to contract, scarlet fever, somewhere in between France and Fort Davens, the stateside camp he arrived at before making the final leg of his journey back to Springfield. This was particularly frustrating for his father, who was forced to give up working during a three-week quarantine period, when no person was allowed to have any contact with any of the Templeton Family for fear of spreading the disease around town, which was the last thing the town needed, having just dealt with the influenza epidemic back in the fall. Even though, the doctor in town strongly recommended that the Templetons take up residence elsewhere to keep from contracting and spreading the disease, they both chose to continue living in the house with their son and simply hope for the best. As a healthy distraction, the Glee Club from Middlebury College came to town and gave a concert. However, the happiness would be short-lived because the dreaded influenza was about to make another appearance in town, crimping everyone's lifestyle and daily activities once again.

Just when it seemed as though, things were about to return to normal for the first time since the United States originally entered the Great War, that ghastly disease known as influenza, chose to rear its ugly head in Springfield one last time. Also, Lawrence Reed, came down with the disease for a second time as well and again probably picked it up at work, just like he did when he came down with it the first time, back in the fall. Gladys, even though she had already been through this disease with her husband once before, didn't mean that she was any more prepared for it this time as compared to when she was confronted with it back in the fall. In her letter to her sister, Edna, Gladys confided that the influenza was "the filthiest disease(with) such an awful discharge from the head and throat" and if she had a choice, she personally would have rather suffered from scarlet fever as opposed to the flu, which is kind of strange, considering that she had been very lucky not to contract either disease, especially having been in close proximity to people with both diseases in the recent weeks.[252] Even though, the doctor told Lawrence that he should remain in bed while he was sick, Lawrence found that the best medicine was continuing to move around and follow his daily routine and schedule as close to normal as possible. As such, Lawrence only ended up missing two days of work, having contracted the disease on Sunday, March 16th and having gone back to work the following Wednesday.

Along with all the flowers, especially geraniums, and the melting of the snow, which brings the Black River to levels which cause it to flood it banks, the arrival of spring also meant the departure of influenza from the region and the return of normalcy to the lives of many of the people in Springfield and the surrounding towns. By the middle of April and after a month of being closed due to the reappearance of the influenza epidemic, the library, the movie theater, the churches and schools have all reopened for normal day to day and week to week activities; and the entire town just prayed that nothing more about influenza got heard ever again.

As spring rolled towards summer, Lawrence and Gladys kept themselves busy with many of the regular day to day activities around the house which for Gladys included sewing projects and housework, while for Lawrence, it meant canning fruits and vegetables and working in the family garden which was up the road from where the Reeds lived and was a holdover from the garden which the neighborhood started during the Great War, when there were food shortages as a result of more store products going overseas to keep the soldiers well fed and able to fight.

June would prove to be a very busy month for the Reeds. When Lawrence was not at the shop working his machine, he more often than not could be found working in the family garden planting and tending to the many vegetables and flowers which included tomatoes, potatoes, endives and radishes for vegetables[253] as well as roses, geraniums, asters and petunias for flowers.[254]

This was also the month where Evelyn made daily progress in maturity as she walked on her own while also growing both her vocabulary and her palette on a daily basis. Lawrence and Gladys both believed that Evelyn would talk off all her baby fat, even if the only thing she did was greet every person who happened to come by the house.[255] All the working in the garden and housework was making all the Reeds look forward to their family vacation at the end of July, during a week, when Bryant was going to shut down briefly, due to the lack of work, which in a small way, may have been a sign of things to come and the places where life was going to take the Reeds over the next few years.

With the war having ended the previous November and a significant number of the local men and boys now home from France, the celebration of July 4th in 1919 promised to be an exciting one in cities and towns all across the United States. Along with an elaborate parade with numerous decorative floats, the highlight of the July 4th celebration in Springfield was supposed to be the presence of a World War One trainer aircraft, most likely a Curtiss JN-4 "Jenny", which the people in town would be able to get rides in for $1 per minute per passenger. However, all the excitement surrounding this aircraft was short-lived, when the plane crashed while giving its first ride of the day, probably due to some less than perfect weather conditions and despite being flown by an experienced, battle tested aviator Edward A. Terhume of Swampscott, Massachusetts. July also marked the first time which Lawrence and Gladys chose to take Evelyn to church on Sunday, during which she attracted a lot of attention from the other members of the congregation. Along with canning their own fruits and vegetables, Lawrence and Gladys also canned fruits and vegetables which they bought from their neighbors, like in July, when the raspberries were ripe for the picking, the Reeds canned six pints of them, which they had purchased for twenty-five cents a quart. Gladys would then spend the following week cleaning the house top to bottom, ahead of them leaving for their family vacation on July 19th to visit Gladys's family in Feeding Hills, Massachusetts and Lawrence's family in New Haven, Connecticut during the week which Lawrence was going to have off from work at Bryant as a result of a lack of work orders following the end of the Great War.

Upon returning from their vacation, one of the first things, Gladys found herself doing was taking Evelyn to the "Little Light Bearer's Party" at the Methodist church in Springfield in which the Reeds were active participants in numerous ways. This party was an opportunity for the church to celebrate its youngest members, specifically those who were five years of age and younger, by bringing them and their mothers together for a special event on a summer's evening. The party was also a type of indoctrination ceremony for the young members of the church's congregation, based on chapter 5, verses 13 to 16, of the Gospel according to Matthew, in which Matthew interprets Jesus's teaching regarding how his followers should behave and be examples to the world and to each other. According to Matthew, Jesus is telling his followers to let their good deeds be a light unto the world and should not get hidden from their fellow men, but rather they should shine out so that they will be known to both man and the divine. The Little Light Bearer's Party was each child's initial introduction to this teaching, which was one of the first sets of verses, the children who were in Sunday school were expected to memorize.

The rest of the summer turned out to be a very busy one for the Reeds between Lawrence working either at the machine shop or in the garden, numerous visits from family and friends and some work being done on the house they lived in on Furnace Street. By the beginning of August, the Reeds were beginning to enjoy many of the fruits and vegetables they had planted in their garden, including peas, summer squash and string beans with cucumbers and tomatoes coming along shortly thereafter. Gladys also received visits from several of her friends from normal school, while Lawrence's sister, Leona, came to stay with them for a few weeks towards the end of the summer and while she was there helped them gather and can apples, blueberries, blackberries and string beans. Also, by summer's end, both apartments in the house on Furnace Street would have a new piazza built on the front of them.

If the Springfield community had a black eye upon it, it was the colored, but mostly negative attitude it held towards its residents of Polish heritage and background, which was really an outgrowth of anti-Catholic sentiment which had roots going back multiple centuries. According to John Tracy Ellis, in his book, American Catholicism, this negative sentiment towards Polish and other southern and eastern European immigrants to the United States was a "universal anti-Catholic bias (which) was brought to Jamestown in 1607 and (was) vigorously cultivated in all thirteen colonies from Massachusetts to Georgia."[256] In other words, the deepest roots of anti-Catholicism in the Americas was directly caused by the fact that the majority of the colonists were of a British Protestant background, whose negative feelings towards Catholicism could arguably be traced all the way back to 1534 when King Henry VIII set off the English Reformation by breaking the Church of England away from the control of the Vatican and the Catholic Church, following the Pope's rejection of Henry's request for a divorce from Catherine of Aragon. The two other root causes which the anti-Catholic and in turn, anti-Polish sentiment can be attributed to in Springfield in the 1910s were the conflicting views Protestants and Catholics had regarding prohibition in the United States with the Protestants for it and the Catholics opposed, as well as the presence of the Ku Klux Klan (KKK) in the region at that time, a group which targeted many non-white, non-protestant groups in the United States, including Blacks, Jews, and Catholics among others. In fact, when another house on Furnace Street came up for auction in August 1919 and when the Reeds' upstairs neighbors, the Dashners, bought it just to keep a polish family from getting their hands in it, Lawrence, at the time, was overheard saying that Mr. Dashner deserved a gold medal for buying it and keeping a Polish family out of the neighborhood. Mrs. Dashner, who staunchly disagreed with her husband's actions, was known to have said that no one would ever fully, if at all, appreciate this act of ethnic and religious discrimination.[257] What makes Lawrence's comments about Polish-Americans so perplexing is that, some of his best customers when it came to the people who purchased the vegetables he put out for sale at the end of the summer, in particular cucumbers, were the town's residents who were of a polish heritage. It just seems odd that he would have such negative things to say about some other people in town and yet when it came to selling them the produce he had put out for sale, as long as their money was green and American, Lawrence was more than happy to do business with them, no matter what their ethnic or religious background may have been.

As August rolled into September, life for the Reeds continued at a rather dizzying pace. Since the schools which, Gladys's friends from normal school taught at, were not opening their doors until the middle of the month, this gave Gladys more opportunities to entertain and visit with her former classmates ahead of their respective first days of classes. She and Lawrence also received a visit from an old childhood friend, George Blackburn, who was a singer with the Guy Brothers' Minstrels, which was traveling around the country at this time and put on a performance in Springfield on September 2nd.[258] Lawrence volunteered to babysit Evelyn in order to allow Gladys, Edna and Gladys's good friend, Margaret, go to the minstrel show, where they saw George sing both as a solo artist and in a quartet, while also going "black face" for the last act of the evening. Fortunately, Lawrence was able was to go to movies on the fourth, the White River Junction Fair on the fifth and to Claremont on the sixth. While Gladys's sister Edna, did the babysitting for Evelyn when everyone else went to the movies and to Claremont; everyone, including Evelyn, was able to attend the White River Junction Fair, during which they were able to watch an airship take off.

Unfortunately, life, even nearly a year after the end of the Great War, was not always easy. Even ten months after the Armistice, products, such as granulated white sugar, were at times hard to come by. Fortunately, brown sugar was readily available and could be used as a substitute in many of the dishes people would make on a regular basis. By the second week of September, Lawrence and Gladys's guests were beginning to head home. Gladys's friend, Margaret left on September 10th, with the beginning of her school year only days away, while Edna would head back to Feeding Hills the following Wednesday in order to tend to her tobacco crop which was just about ready to be cut down and harvested.[259] Aside from making a couple additional trips to Lakes Rescue and Echo as well as the West River Creamery in Londonderry, Vermont, Gladys and Lawrence, when he wasn't working at the machine shop, spent their time canning tomatoes and tending to the garden. By month's end, they had canned twenty seven quarts, one pint and eight cans of tomatoes along with three cans of corn. The rest of the vegetables were sold to the locals, with two bushels of green tomatoes costing $1.25 per bushel, a half bushel of ripe tomatoes costing $1.50 per bushel and $0.75 for a bushel of cucumbers. The $4.75 for those aforementioned vegetables was enough money to cover all the costs for the garden, including the seeds for the vegetables and flowers as well as the cost of the materials to tend the garden. Even though 1919 was well on its way to being a tough year for the machine shops in the Springfield area, given the number of canceled defense orders as a result of the conclusion of World War One, Lawrence Reed had many reasons to feel good going into the first anniversary of the signing of the Armistice and the subsequent holiday season because, starting in October, Lawrence's pay rate was set to increase $1.50 per week,[260] while also being one of the few fortunate individuals to keep his job at Bryant Chucking Grinder, as the majority of the shop's operations shifted to making automotive and aircraft parts, following the cancellation of all the orders for ammunition shells by the United States Department of Defense.

As summer turned to fall in 1919 and the leaves of the trees began to change colors, many Americans looked towards the upcoming holiday season, with the hopes that they would be able to celebrate Thanksgiving and Christmas with all their loved ones, and not have to wonder about the safety and welfare of the soldiers and nurses who were overseas on the front lines of battle. However, President Woodrow Wilson wanted to make sure that the sacrifices and efforts made by the nation's soldiers, nurses and stateside workers, such as the machinists, would not get overlooked or forgotten. To do this, Wilson authored and signed a proclamation, which would appear in many newspapers across country and declared November 11th to be a day on which Americans should celebrate the efforts and roles, each and every one of them played, along with those of their European compatriots, in ensuring a victory which allowed "new possibilities of political freedom and economic concert"[261] to arise, while showing the world how a nation could remodel its industries, concentrate its financial resources, increase its agricultural output and assemble a great army to be a decisive factor in the Allies' victory over the Central Powers.[262] A sentiment which President Dwight D. Eisenhower would extend to all American soldiers and service personnel when he ordered Armistice Day be renamed Veterans Day in 1954 in honor of all those who had served their country since its founding in 1776.

Afterword

When I began the research for this book, little did I realize the journey it would take me on. What began as a search for a single letter led to a box of letters, turned into a comprehensive college essay and then into the book you have in your hands. From stories about my maternal great-grandparents' everyday lives to how the Great War impacted every individual soldier and civilian, I hope this book was able to paint a picture of what 1910s New England was like during World War One. However, until I got the other half of their correspondence from my great aunt, the ability to create such an in-depth story about her parents' lives and where they lived in the late 1910s was almost impossible. By beginning the project with only one side of the correspondence, the fruits and pitfalls of primary source research, both became very apparent. By having both halves of my maternal great-grandparents' correspondence, particularly from years during which they were courting, a very clear picture of the lives of two young Americans during the days and months leading up to and just after the United States declared war on Germany on April 6, 1917, began to take shape.

Lastly, I want to take one final opportunity to thank all of the individuals who played a role, whether big or small, in the successful completion of this book. First off, I would like to thank my family, each of whom played a part in locating and/or verifying many of the personal and familial stories in the book. Next, my contacts in Springfield, Vermont, especially those at the Springfield Arts and Historical Society (SAHS), who's willingness to assist me in locating some of the local and regional material in the book proved invaluable. Lastly, I would like to thank my two advisors from the University of Connecticut, who's desire to oversee the college essay aspect of this process cannot be understated, especially that of Professor Yael Schacher, who has continued to assist me in an editorial and advisory role above and beyond the completion of the coursework during which this book began to take shape. Just like the efforts of soldiers and civilians were both necessary members of the team which led to the American Expeditionary Force's success on the front lines; I am very thankful for every member of my team and the role he or she played during the research and completion of my book.

World War One Advertisements, Literature and Posters

Liberty Bonds and War Savings Stamps

"Everyone is expected to do their bit"

Our first subscription to the United States Government "Liberty Loan" was $100,000.00.

We are now ready to send in another subscription.

Kindly hand us yours as soon as possible.

No expense to you.

First National Bank
Springfield, Vermont
Bank Closes Saturdays at 12:30.

Springfield Reporter, May 11, 1917

United States of America
"Liberty Loan of 1917"

"To such a task we can dedicate our lives and our fortunes, everything that we are, and everything that we have, with the pride of those who know that the day has come when America is privileged to spend her blood and her might for the principles that gave her birth and happiness, and the peace which she has treasured."

President Wilson's Message to Congress,
April 2, 1917

We are subscribing for a substantial amount of these bonds for our own account and we urge you to subscribe.

First National Bank
Springfield, Vermont
Bank Closes Saturdays at 12:30.

Springfield Reporter, June 1, 1917

The People of Springfield Subscribed $304,000 of the Liberty Loan of 1917

which was 2½ times their allotment.

Those who bought Liberty Bonds of us, please call and receive their Liberty button.

First National Bank
Springfield, Vermont
Bank Closes Saturdays at 12:30.

Springfield Reporter, June 21, 1917

$5,000,000,000
Needed for the Army and Navy

It is the duty and privilege of all loyal citizens to make the contemplated

New Government War Loan

a tremendous success. Our country needs the help of each and every true American

We take pleasure in placing our facilities at the disposal of the Public for the purpose of receiving subscriptions to this issue, whenever and in whatever form authorized by the Government, without profit or commission of any kind whatsoever.

First National Bank
Springfield, Vermont

Springfield Reporter, 1917

Springfield Reporter, April 18, 1918

Springfield Reporter, April 4, 1918

Buying Line or Firing Line

YOU must stand in one or the other or lose the respect of your neighbors and go down the gloriously reconstructive years accompanied by the public and private knowledge that you were a slacker in the time which tested the manhood and womanhood of the world.

If you have bought Liberty Bonds of the three preceding loans you will need no urging to

Join the Fighting Fourth

Lend as the boys in France fight—to the utmost. Don't carp at the rate of interest, don't criticize your Government, don't hoard, don't spend unnecessarily.

Buy Liberty Bonds today—at any bank—cash or instalments

**Save to Buy
and
Buy to Keep**

Liberty Loan Committee
of New England

This Advertisement is Endorsed and Paid for by the FIRST NATIONAL BANK as a Part of Their Efforts to Fight This War to a Prompt and Victorious Conclusion.

Springfield Reporter, October 3, 1918

Enlist as a war saver in the great "army that stays at home"—the *second line* of defense behind our boys in the first line trenches.

The government has officially set Friday, June 28th, as

National War Savings Day

Be ready to step forward on that day and prove your patriotism. Don't wait to be summoned to "sign the pledge"—arrange now to invest in a definite amount of War Savings Stamps each month during 1918.

W. S. S. Cost $4.17 in June
Worth $5.00 Jan. 1st, 1923

Be Ready to Go the Limit—Line Up and Sign Up on June 28th

National War Savings Committee

This space contributed for the Winning of the War by

BRYANT CHUCKING GRINDER COMPANY

Springfield Reporter, June 20, 1918

THE fighting slogan in France, gathering inspiration and significance as the conflict grows more violent and more desperate, is "Carry On." On land, on sea, in the air, it rings sharp and clear.

Into the front line trenches comes the signal to charge. The company commander swings "over the top." At his heels, pushing and stumbling through the hell of "No Man's Land," come the boys. They gain a yard, five, ten, and the machine guns speak. The commander falls, but over his shoulder, above the din of battle, he shouts, "Carry On, Lieutenant!" So on and on, till every officer falls, and the grizzled old Sergeant sets his teeth and takes what's left of them on to victory.

"Carry On" must be our slogan here at home. We must "Carry On" to the utmost limit our ability, to the last dollar of our resources, till *Victory* is won. Let us stand shoulder to shoulder—*buy* all the Liberty Bonds we can. Let us *keep* our Bonds and *save* to buy more.

"Carry On!" Buy Liberty Bonds!

THIS SPACE SUBSCRIBED TO WINNING THE WAR BY

CAHEE HOUSE FURNISHING COMPANY

Springfield Reporter, October 3, 1918

Generations of true Americans have carried the flag to victory in just warfare. Now it is our turn to keep the flag flying before the world's struggling masses who are battling to keep liberty's flame alive in the hearts of men.

New England will not fail to help. The birth-place of freedom has ever been true to its ideals.

The Fighting Fourth Liberty Loan will be sold September 28 — October 19. The amount will be greater — the time shorter. The money is absolutely required to seal the fruits of a victorious beginning. More men, more ships, more guns, more planes are needed to form and equip our rapidly growing army and win the war. Save to buy more Liberty Bonds than ever before.

The Fighting Fourth

Has a place for everyone in its ranks. Men, women and children can all buy bonds. They can be bought at any bank, for cash or on partial payments. Get ready now and be the first patriot to join the *Fighting Fourth*.

Save to Buy
and
Buy to Keep

*Buy as the boys in France fight —
to the utmost*

Liberty Loan Committee
of New England

Springfield Reporter, October 3, 1918

Springfield Reporter, October 10, 1918

Mighty Unpleasant Work, this—

Save
to
Buy
—
Buy
to
Keep

BUT have you heard of any Yankee soldier shirking his job?

Hardly! The things our boys have done "over there," both at the front and behind the lines, make us rejoice in the fact that we are Americans.

When *they* get the report of the present "Liberty Loan Drive" will they, too, rejoice?

They will if we do our manifest duty, and "*we*" includes *you*, as well as all the rest of us.

The fourth issue Liberty Loan is "The Fighting Fourth." We can't all join the boys in bayonet work, but—

We can at least back 'em to the "last ditch" with our "fighting dollars."

Buy bonds the way our boys in France fight—to the utmost

Buy today—at any bank—cash or instalments

Liberty Loan Committee of New England

Springfield Reporter, October 3, 1918

10 cents

Of Every Dollar in Cash Sales on

Thursday and Friday
May 3d and 4th

will go to the Treasury of the local
Red Cross Chapter

The "Red Cross Days" have the approval and support of the officers of the chapter

Plan to do your shopping these two days and help a worthy cause

IT PAYS TO PAY CASH — QUALITY-SERVICE
Houghton & Simonds
SPRINGFIELD — and — BRATTLEBORO

Springfield Reporter,
April 27, 1917

"Put Vermont Behind the Fighting Man"

The Vermont State Chapter of the American Red Cross will conduct a State-wide membership campaign May 28 to June 2 inclusive for

30,000 New Members in Vermont

Red Cross is the only volunteer-relief organization authorized by the government. By joining the Red Cross you help the wounded soldier and sailor. If you can't fight, you can help. Back up the fighting forces with your membership.

Join Your Red Cross

CLASSES OF MEMBERSHIP	
Subscribing member, $2.00 a year	Life member, $25.00 (once)
Contributing member, $5.00 a year	Patron life $100.00 (once)
Sustaining member, $10.00 a year	Annual member $1.00 a year
Monthly Magazine included in all except Annual Membership	

Send Your Membership to Your Local Branch or to Red Cross Headquarters, Burlington, Vermont.

Springfield Reporter,
May 25, 1917

Your Privilege and Your Duty

Don't ask the fighting man to do it all; get back of him with your help in a practical way.

Join Your Red Cross

and be one of the 30,000 new members in the Vermont Chapter who will contribute their small membership fee this week toward the work of the only volunteer relief organization authorized by the government.

Don't Wait---Join To-Day

CLASSES OF MEMBERSHIP	
Subscribing member, $2.00 a year	Life member, $25.00 (once)
Contributing member, $5.00 a year	Patron life $100.00 (once)
Sustaining member, $10.00 a year	Annual member $1.00 a year
Monthly Magazine included in all except Annual Membership	

Send Your Membership to Your Local Branch or to Red Cross Headquarters, Burlington, Vermont.

Springfield Reporter,
June 1, 1917

Vermont's Bit
$200,000

Toward the $100,000,000 Fund to be raised for the

AMERICAN RED CROSS

Our Vermont Soldiers are going to fight for you—give liberally toward this Red Cross Fund

Vermont's Great Membership Campaign Pleased Everybody

Vermont will Again Make Good with $200,000

This big-money campaign begins on Monday, June 18th, with every Red Cross Member determined to make it the greatest Red Cross success that has ever taken place.

7 DAYS OF EFFORT 7

7 DAYS TO RAISE $200,000

Campaign Headquarters, BURLINGTON, 196 Main Street. VERMONT

Springfield Reporter,
June 14, 1917

Food and Entertainment

Full Line of Canned Goods

Peas, Corn, Succotash, Beans, Spinach, Asparagus Tips, Pears, Raspberries, Peaches, Pineapples and Plums.

Springfield Market Co.
Telephone 130

Springfield Reporter, April 3, 1917

We Have
New Maple Sugar and Syrup
It's Fine

Special Bargains in Canned Goods This Week

Try Our Bread and Cake Cheaper than you can make it

Our Sales Increase Every Month

Are You Using Stearns Bros. Best Coffee?
If Not, Try a Pound, It's Fine

STEARNS BROS.
The TEA and COFFEE STORE

Springfield Reporter, April 3, 1917

Canned
Fruits and Preserves

Canned Before Sugar Went Up

We Give You the Benefit

Peaches	Pineapples
Raspberries	Blueberries
Plums	

Loganberry, Raspberry, Blackberry Preserves

Home-Made Jellies

Lovell's Market
Three free deliveries daily   Phone 17

Springfield Reporter, May 4, 1917

The Price of Flour
is Steadily Advancing

"A word to the wise——"

Springfield Reporter, May 11, 1917

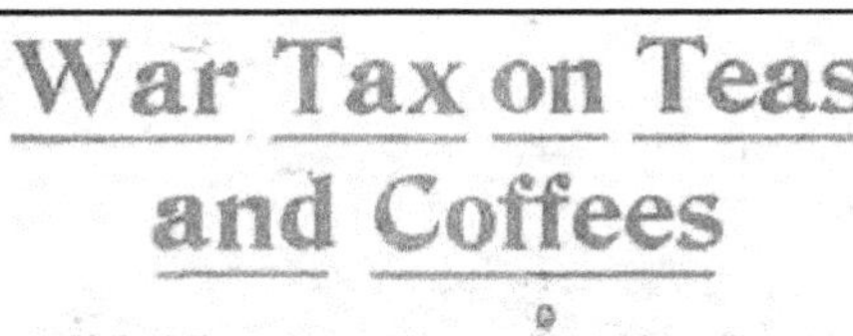

Springfield Reporter, June 8, 1917

Springfield Reporter, July 5, 1917

Springfield Reporter,
October 18, 1917

Springfield Reporter,
September 26, 1917

Seeds

3000 Bushels Japanese Buckwheat

The Ideal Emergency Crop

LARGE STOCKS

Barley, Oats, Rye, Sudan, Hungarian, Millet, Field Peas, Cow Peas, Soy Beans, Pea Beans, Yellow Eye Beans, Field Corn, Fodder Corn. All for quick shipment.

The Holbrook Grocery Co.

Wholesale Distributors
Keene, N. H. and Woodsville, N. H.

Springfield Reporter, June 14, 1917

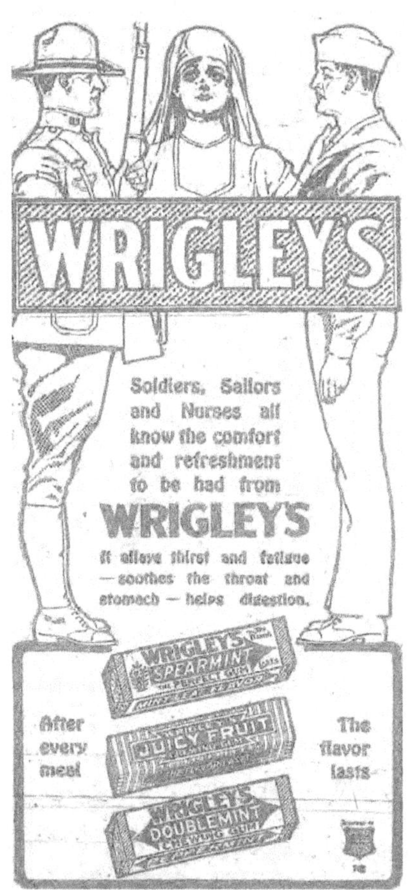

Springfield Reporter, Sepetember 27, 1917

Begining Saturday Morning

The Prices on all Spring Coats and Suits
will be Changed in Your Favor

Don't Buy Until You See Our Stock

About 50 Very Desirable Garments

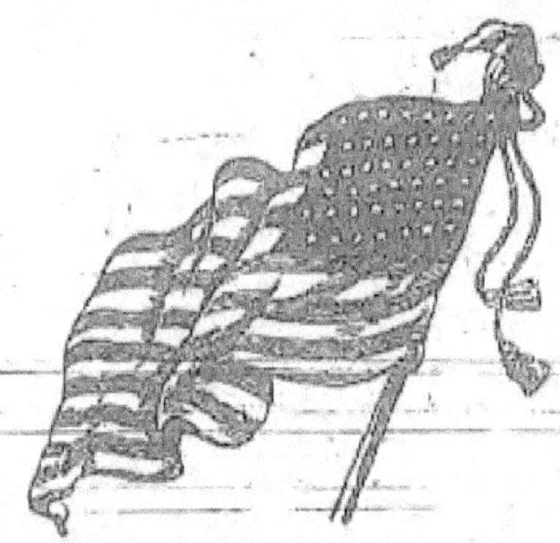

R. M. WILCOMB & CO.

Springfield Reporter, May 25, 1917

"THE GROUND GRIPPER"
SURGICAL SHOE

is the Original Muscle Developing Health Shoe

Everyone who enjoys walking, or has to stand on their feet most of the time, will find this shoe a source of rest, and a practical cure for foot troubles.

COMFORT FOR ALL FEET

C. H. MOORE, The Shoeman

Springfield Reporter, May 18, 1917

Springfield Reporter, October 3, 1917

Springfield Reporter, October 3, 1917

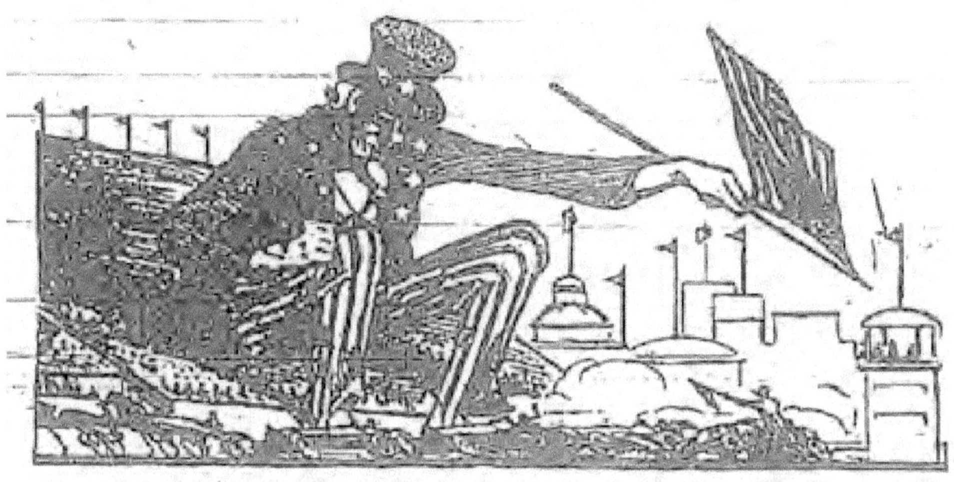

Springfield Reporter, October 11, 1917

Springfield Reporter, October 3, 1917

Springfield Reporter, October 3, 1917

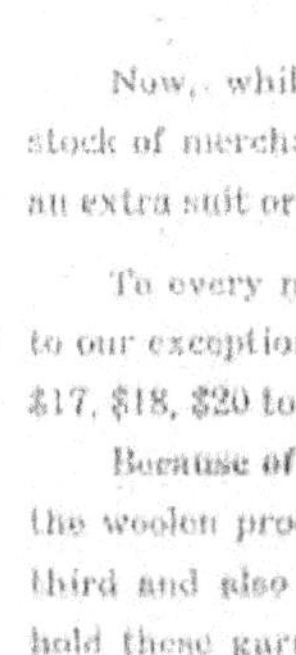

Springfield Reporter, October 3, 1917

Springfield Reporter, January 10, 1918

World War One Era Posters

"Our Boys Need Sox... Knit Your Bit"
American Lithographic Co., 1917

"Be Patriotic"
W.F. Powers Co., 1918

"Get Behind the Girl he left behind him. Join the Land Army"
American Lithographic Co., 1918

**"Registered War Garden Under
Protection of State Council of Defense"**
J.N. Dingo. Barnes-Crosby Co., 1918

"Your Sugar Ration is 2 lbs. per month"
U.S. Food Administration, 1917

"**V – Liberty Loan**", 1917

"Gee!! I Wish I Were a Man. I'd Join the Navy."
Howard Chandler Christy, 1918

"United Behind the Service Star"
United War Work Campaign. Ernest Hamlin Baker, 1918

"United War Work Campaign – Week of November 11, 1918"
Alco-Gravure, Inc., 1918

A Little Literature

The Battle Hymn of Democracy

By Edward S. Van Zile

What hear we in the world today?
The thunder of the guns,
Their rumbling and grumbling, and the pathway of the suns
Is echoing with wailings as the women find their dead;
And there's shrieking of the shrapnel where the grass is turning red.
But there's music! Don't you hear it?
'Tis a hymn the nations sing,
As their spirit calls to spirit,
And they crown the People King.
'Tis a Marseillaise so wonderful
That all the world's awake
To the story of the glory
That is won for Freedom's sake.
Ah, the groaning and the moaning
And the price the dying pay!
The earth is rent with anguish,
But there was no other way!
But, lo, the light is coming and a mighty chorus rings
That stirs our souls to gladness,
And to sadness those of kings,
They know who sit upon their thrones
The menace of the song;
They played at dice with human bones,
And all the world went wrong.
And ages after ages they mocked at God, and said
That nations were but toys for them, the living and the dead.
But there's music! Don't you hear it,
Where the East and West have met,
And the people cry for justice,
And the monarchs pay their debt?
Where ocean calls to ocean
And where mountains haunt the sky,
The day has come when Truth shall live
And ancient Error die.
'Tis a Marseillaise so marvelous
The Earth is singing now—
As the peoples find their power and fulfill a sacred vow—
That the stars that dance along the sky
Its rhythm seem to feel
And the universe is throbbing
With glad, triumphant peal.
Ye dead who paid the price for us,
Your name shall never die;
But kings shall be forgotten
In the splendid bye-and-bye;
And from a world's Democracy,
That's born of blood and woe,
A harvest shall be garnered
From the seed our heroes sow.
What hear we in the world today?
A paean wild and sweet,
The People's song of victory;
And where the nations meet
Not king shall call to brother king,
But race shall speak to race;
And man, no longer slave to man,
Shall look God in the face!

—The Milwaukee Journal.

"A Patriot's Creed", 1918

World War One Era Letters

Topic	From	To	Date	Page
Armistice Day	Gladys Reed	Edna Steere	Nov 17, 1918	175
Short War Hopes	Gladys Reed	Lawrence Reed	Apr 15, 1917	182
Honeymoon	Lawrence / Gladys	Edna Steere	Jun 28, 1917	190
Shortages / Rationing	Carrie Merchant	Gladys Reed	Feb 4, 1918	196
First Child	Lawrence / Gladys	Edna Steere	Mar 23, 1918	205
Theodore Roosevelt	Edna Steere	Gladys Reed	May 2, 1918	209
July 4th	Gladys Reed	Edna Steere	Jul 6, 1919	217

The Armisitice Day Letter

Springfield, VT

Nov. 17, 1918

Dear Edna,

Hasn't this been a lovely day? Seems as though it would make a good tobacco damp if it's as warm down there as it is here. We haven't done much of anything. Lawrence went to Sunday School and I cooked chicken for dinner.

Yesterday afternoon Lawrence cut wood and it was so warm that I washed the car for him. It was quite an undertaking for it was awfully dirty but we don't like to put it up for the winter call covered with mud.

I suppose you took in the peace celebration in the city. They had quite a lively and noisy time here. The men all quit work at 9 a.m. so of course they had to do something. The shops had a parade and made a pretty good showing. I was surprised that there were not more automobiles out considering the number there are in town. The whistles and bells started their noise at 7:30 a.m. and kept it up all day. I was in the midst of a good big washing so I didn't feel a whole lot like celebrating. But when Lawrence came home we soon got the washing out. We went down to the corner of the street to see the parade and after that we started for Westminster to get the potatoes we bought. They were just having their parade in Bellows Falls so we had to dodge around the side streets to get out their way. But after all their celebrating the papers don't seem to feel sure that the Germans are through.

I saw the things Wilfred Dashner sent to his folks for Christmas. Cigar holders for Fred and his father and collars to Ethel and his mother. The collars are of net with a braided pattern on them. They are hand made and very neat and pretty. Of course they seem pretty fine because they came all the way from

France. Have you happened to see the size of the box that they are allowed to send the boys across? Just about the size of a Uneeda biscuit box. I don't know what they think one can send in such an insignificant thing but I suppose there are so many that they have to cut them down some.

We are all well. Perhaps you would like to know that Miss Evelyn is standing up. She stands up in her carriage to perfection but much to our discomfort. I put her on the floor but there is nothing the right height for her to hold on to there. I guess she will be walking in another *month if she doesn't break her neck in the meantime.*

I have the piano in the dining room now. It was rather hard to heat the parlor so we put the china closet in the parlor, put the buffet where the china closet was and the piano is in the place where the buffet was. I don't know just how we can manage when we get our stove in the dining room but guess we'll put the buffet where the sewing machine is and the sewing machine between the two windows.

She had a coal fire all the week till Friday. It wasn't livable in the house with one that day so we let it out and haven't had

month if she doesn't break her neck in the meantime.

I have the piano in the dining room now. It was rather hard to heat the parlor so we put the china closet in the parlor, put the buffet where the china closet was. I don't know just how we can manage when we get our stove in the dining room but guess we'll put the buffet where the sewing machine is and the sewing machine between the two windows.

We had a coal fire all the week till Friday. It wasn't livable in the house with one that day so we let it out and haven't had but a little wood fire since.

Well, it's only a little over a week before Thanksgiving. We ought to stay at home and save the twelve dollars it will cost for car fare but probably we won't get down there again this winter so we may as well make the most of the opportunity. We haven't quite

decided yet but think we'll take the train that leaves Charlestown at 4 p.m. That won't make us so very late if we connect well with the trolleys. I'll tell you more definitively when I write next time.

I almost forgot to tell you

a most startling piece of news. You can believe it or not as Mrs. Templeton told it to me. Fred Dashner has joined the Episcopal church at Charlestown. I think probably it's a fact because Mrs. Dashner has been very sober all the week. He joined a week ago today. Guess if that's the case they won't be living with the old folks much longer.

I must close as it's nearing bedtime.

Love to all,

Gladys

The Short War Hopes Letter

Middlefield, MA

April 15, 1917

My own dearest Larry,

Poor Larry, what can I do or say that will cheer you up? If I could only see you for a little while perhaps I could encourage you a little bit. But, you mustn't get so down hearted. It isn't good for you. I hardly think that you will ever have to enlist by my making you and I don't believe that this country will resort to drafting. I surely hope not anyway. We certainly struck a very troubled time to get married but I guess everything will be quiet and peaceable before long. It seems to me that we have been deprived of our happiness quite long enough. Of course it's hard to tell what may happen but let's hope for the best. If we had known as much two months ago as we know now we could have got married during vacation. I have wished more than once during the last three weeks that we had. I don't know as it would be much consolation but it would help some to know that we really do belong to each other if you should have to go away for any length of time. If you would be any happier married, just say so, for you know, dear, that I am perfectly willing to do anything possible to please you. Of course, I want to finish my year out up here but if you would get any consolation from the fact that we really are married, always to belong to each other, I'm perfectly willing and ready to say the word. Sometimes I think that I would like to leave this place forever and take the first train I could that will take me to you, and then – well I decide that there are only ten more weeks so I can endure it. Then I think if we were only married it would help some to think that I really have the dearest and best hubby on earth who is ready and willing to do anything for me. Then again I sometimes think that we are as well off now as we ever can be till we can be together, happy and contented in our own home. It's a rather hard problem, but remember, dearest Larry that I am more than willing to do anything I can that will make you happy. I love you so much that I will give up almost anything to please you.

It is still cold and wintry up this way but I guess summer will get here after a while although it seems a long way off. I don't do very much now-a-days. I seem to have lost my ambition but here's hoping that it will be found again soon. Perhaps the change of air had a bad effect on me.

If you think you could love me enough to cheer me up I wish you were right here now. I would be perfectly all right, I'm sure, if I could only rest in your arms tonight and let you kiss me just as often as you please. It would be perfect bliss but oh dear! what's the use of talking about your being here when I know perfectly well you can't be. I'm lonesome and I want you oh! so bad right now, nobody knows how much but you, dear.

I tried to be good as I went to church this morning. Did you go? Gertrude leads the Christian Endeavour tonight so I suppose I shall have to go to see that she does it properly. I haven't any excuse for not going as Steve isn't here to take care of now. My, how I wish he was! He kept me from getting lonesome a great many times but he's gone so the sooner I forget him the better it will be.

I guess that the folks down home have forgotten all about me for I haven't heard a word from them since I came back. They don't like to write letters any better than you do.

The Christian Endeavour topic for tonight is about how we

should keep the Sabbath. I asks if it is right to write letters on Sunday, if it's right to ride in autos for pleasure, and to go for a walk on

Sunday. If it's wrong to write letters just think of how many times we have done wrong. As for riding in autos I guess I won't say or walking either for we should have a terrible heap of sins piled up.

I don't know of anything else to write so I will close for this time. Try to cheer up, dear, and everything will be all right before long.

Yours forever, dearest Larry, with all my love and lots of kisses,

Glad.

The Honeymoon Letter

June 28, 1917

Dear Edna,

We just sent you a card a little while ago to let you know where we are. We didn't intend to stay here tonight but expected to go on to Syracuse. However, just as we were leaving we heard our little Ford begin to groan. We decided it must be sick so it is in the garage until tomorrow a.m.

We have had a very enjoyable time so far but we are a little bit afraid of rain tomorrow.

We left Springfield at 1:20 p.m. yesterday and came as far as Amsterdam last night, a distance of about 125 miles. We rode about 60 miles today and have been here since the middle of the afternoon. It's a large city with lots going on. We took in a show this afternoon "Beware of Strangers". Quite a bit of good advice in it. It seems that all plays now-a-days have a very marked moral.

I wish that you could be with us to see all the country out this way. It is quite different from Massachusetts. The land isn't mountainous but somewhat rolling. It would do the men folks good to see the farms out through here. They are laid out in fine shape and all the crops are planted so as to have the rows as straight as can be. It is fine with beautiful scenery.

We follow the Erie Canal for most of the way across the state. It isn't very wonderful to see

except the places where it winds over solid rock. We have a picture of one of the locks so you can see how it looks. Lawrence said that it is too bad that you and Bertha aren't with us to hold down the back seat. He is afraid that Ma might get tired if she tried to ride so far in one day as we do.

I don't believe that you would have enjoyed riding over Manchester Mountain. It is in the western part of Vermont and I assure you that Middlefield isn't in it at all in comparison.

We coasted down for between 2 and 3 miles and it's full of water bars. It was quite a stunt to come down but it will be more of a one to get up it again.

I'll try to send you a card from wherever we are tomorrow but we don't always strike the part of a town or city where we can find cards.

I've gone completely crazy over Springfield. It's a dandy town, up hill and down but it's great. When you come up I know we'll have to send you home because you'll like it so well you'll want to stay right there.

Our house is great and the furnishings are better yet.

I also wish you could see our room here tonight. Some class to us, I tell you. This is a new hotel. Judging from the expenses it must be the Kimball of Utica.

Last night we staid at the Warner in Amsterdam. That was very nice but this is better yet: brass bed, bathroom all to ourselves, telephone, etc. Perhaps we shall find it hard to settle down in one place after all this travelling.

Room 223 Martin Hotel, Utica,

N.Y. this is where we are hanging out tonight. Of course this is myself writing beginning with this paragraph. Lawrence of course I should have said. Such a time we are having here today for we don't know which way to turn when we strike a new city. We keep as near the Erie Canal and the Big Four railroad tracks as we can and keep travelling west, many times not knowing where we are at. But it is great fun just the same. Gladys and I have learnt more about auto traveling since we struck York State then we ever knew before in all our previous travels. It is indeed a fine trip over thru these cities and towns for the condition of the country roads and tilled ground is so different from Vermont of Mass.

Gladys says it is bedtime now so of course since I dislike to share the sheets with her I will bring my scribbling to a halt.

With heaps of love,

Gladys & Lawrence

We are expecting to see you and Mrs. Sponable up to Vermont soon. Good night nurse.

The Shortages/Rationing Letter

19 Shattuck St.

Greenfield, Mass.

Feb. 4, 1918

My dear Glad,

Your letter very gladly received last week. Was very glad to hear you were so comfortable in spite of the terrible severe weather and shortage of fuel. Do hope you keep on being comfortable.

Speaking of the sugar shortage we, at home, have not been completely out at any time so but what we had come in the sugar bowl. Lately they have been bringing it in to us every week or two a couple pounds at a time. There have been times when we have had only a pound at a time and even as small a package as half a pound. We sweetened some apple sauce with Karo once and it went very well. We tried making doughnuts with Karo and one trial was enough. We were able to eat them but they seemed tasteless in spite of the fact that we put extra spice into them.

Flour, at present seems to be about the hardest thing to get. You are supposed to buy a certain amount of corn flour now when you buy whcat flour so that your brcad will bc 30% corn flour and later it will be all corn flour. It will seem queer to be obliged to eat those things, won't it? Are you not glad you are not depending on Dickinson Hall to keep you from starving these times? I often wonder what they feed the girls now.

I saw by last week's paper that 14% of the usual number of girls attending Normal are otherwise engaged and that one thousand teachers in Mass. alone have left school service for the government war emergency work.

All the first six grades in town have closed their schools for lack of coal for two weeks or until further notice. All the ninth, eighth and seventh grades are to run and also thru sixth grades in the downtown group. I had to take my school downtown. The ninth, two of the seventh, and two of the sixth grades keep in the morning from 8 until 12. I am in that group. The eighth, remaining seventh, and sixth grades keep in the afternoon from 1 until 5. We have a five minute recess and get along very nicely. We started this new plan today. The Davis St. building where this is being done is a large eight room building. The Davis St. building High School and domestic science cottage, also, the Manual Training building are the only buildings heated in town besides the country schools which have an abundance of fuel.

There is one disadvantage there is no chance to stay after school to put extra work on the board on to help backwards pupils. However I am thankful to teach now instead of in hot weather. However, I would not be at all surprised if schools began in Aug. this next season. The time is coming without doubt when the all year school will be in force. You probably recall it as one of Dr. Snedden's hopes and dreams. Dr. Payson Smith says our schools are demoralizing as a result of the war. Many, many children have left school to earn, and so many teachers have left. Men teachers are getting scarce in the high schools as a lot of them have either enlisted in the Aviation Corps or have gone to Plattsburgh.

It is a very cold blustering day here. The little snow that came yesterday is drifting furiously.

The folks at present have coal enough but if this weather continues it will not last long. They are comfortable considering everything.

Out in Ohio along

the river they are having floods now. It has been prophesied that we will have a heavy damage by water this year.

I suppose ice will be high next summer as it costs so much to harvest it. It has frozen clear to the bottom of the streams and ponds in some places.

Mrs. Davis' son, Murray, got exempted from the draft the other day. He has poor teeth in his lower jaw and a set of false teeth for the upper jaw, consequently, he was thrown out. Gladys's husband passed. He had his examination today.

I thank you very much for your invitation to go to Vermont this summer, of that we will see later. Must close now and go downtown.

Very lovingly, Carrie

P.S. Please remember me to your folks in Feeding Hills. Hope your mother will go to Vt. and get rested.

C.M.M.

The First Child Letter

Springfield, Vt.

March 23, 1918

Dear Edna,

First of all I must tell you what has taken place here at 17 Furnace Street today. We have a 7½ pound baby girl and she is very quiet and good. She came this morning at twenty five minutes past twelve midnight. Gladys had a very easy time of it all and no stitches were taken on her. The doctor came very promptly when I telephoned him at ten o'clock last evening. She is resting very comfortably today I am glad to say. I had a trained nurse at the house here during the time she was needed. The nurse was here till about half past two this morning. She went home when the doctor went home. Everything worked out to perfection and I was surely pleased that I was able to get the nurse as well as the doctor when I needed them so late in the evening. The doctor came this morning again at half past eleven but as Gladys was all right he didn't stay long. The baby sleeps plenty and Gladys sleeps fairly well also. The doctor left some medicine for Gladys to take if she had any pains but thank goodness she hasn't had any so far so the medicine is still where he left it.

Well it is such a joke on us that it turned out to be a girl instead of a boy. Anyhow we are not sorry that it turned out to be a girl. We haven't named the baby yet so I can't tell you her name now.

My mother hasn't got here yet but I hope to have her here this afternoon some time. The nurse has just gone home now at one o'clock. She washed the baby and dressed her again.

Poor Gladys is as hungry as can be and she can only have a few things to eat such as weak tea, milk, toast and liquid foods. It is pretty tough on her for she always eats so heartily usually.

I didn't any more than get undressed when Gladys was taken sick so I hustled into my clothes and I wasn't long getting Dr. Chapman down here you can bet. But Gladys is better today much better in fact than she even believed she ever could be.

Well at last our stove has arrived here.

It was shipped the 28th of February from Kalamazoo, Mich. and it arrived here in about ten days or less. That is it arrived at the express office here at Springfield but the stove company did not put the street address on so the express company here didn't know where to deliver the stove. But this week Monday I found the express clerk and told him where to deliver it and he delivered it Tuesday night. Friday afternoon I had the hot water front connected and it looks fine and acts well so far. The white enamel finish shows off to perfection but I won't say too much about it but you can see it yourself sometime.

Just before I close I'll say what Gladys said.

She says that the baby neither looks like me or herself but rather a third freak. So she says now but we'll know who she resembles later I expect. I'll write you again this week to let you know how she is getting along.

With our love to all,

Lawrence & Gladys

The Theodore Roosevelt Letter

Feeding Hills, Mass.

May 2, 1918

Dear Ma & Gladys,

I have so much riding to do I can hardly find time to write. Howard has been obliged to carry the milk for the last three nights and so I go whether I have the supper dishes washed or not. The Case family have the German Measles and Mr. Case is afraid taking cold if he goes out (a good excuse). Last night, Pa went to hear Roosevelt at the auditorium and Howard carried him way over to the city. I went, too and left Clint and Prince and Minerva to keep house. I had time to get my dishes washed last night. It was showery and it rained hard going over. Of course Howard felt pretty bad to get his car wet and spattered and told Pa it was one of his nights but I don't see that the auto looks very bad today.

Howard has been plowing and harrowing Mr. Hall's garden these last two days and Pa and Clint are planting potatoes. They are taking lots of pains planting them as they want a good crop after paying so much for the seed potatoes.

I don't believe the blood root you saw on the road to Rockingham was any handsomer than yours in the garden for it could not be but probably more of it. I think it is a very pretty ride to Rockingham for I remember I enjoyed it very much last summer. I think Ma took quite a lengthy ride for her.

We can fairly see the things grow down here. Last Tuesday was so warm that the flowers in the garden doubled in size. The shad trees are all in blossom and Mrs. Shea and Cora went picking cow-slips yesterday afternoon. It was too wet for me and I did not want to get another cold.

Mr. Iserman came after his rent this afternoon. He did not come in but visited with Pa in the yard.

I haven't seen Bertha this week. I don't get a chance to go down but shall soon if she don't come up.

They say Barnett is going to keep pigs on his land below our pasture. He has fenced it in with the old picket fence that used to be around the Suffield fair grounds. He is putting it around the part of the lot where the spring is.

Sheas have bought a couple of pigs. They got them from some Polander out Warnertown way. He had no more to spare. Howard says he must take an auto ride and look some up.

I ordered a 24 lb. bag of bread flour today with the substitutes. I am not all out of flour but I wanted some of the substitutes so thought I might as well get the wheat too. I got 10 lbs. of corn flour, 5 of barley, 2 pkges. of corn starch, 2 pounds of rice and the rest of rolled oats. I have got to make bread tonight. I haven't a bit for breakfast so got a small loaf at the store. I made 6 big loaves of oatmeal Monday and I did not realize it was so near gone. I shall make rye bread tonight but next time will try the corn flour.

I have been invited to make some sandwiches for the minister's reception tomorrow night so I suppose I must make a loaf of clear wheat for them. You know

I will enjoy making them. I was a good mind to give them rye ones.

Mrs. Shea brought over a root of her hydrangea tonight and Pa has set it in the new tub. She had it taken up before I knew it or I would not have let her. I think yours is beginning to sprout out from the roots but guess it froze all right. Pa has brought the lilies out of the cellar. They look green.

I went down and picked a bunch of adder-tongues in Iserman's meadow. It was just yellow with them.

Ma has got her check from Orange Judd Company. It came May 1st.

Did you see in your paper that Mamie Harvey is dead? She died Monday eve and was buried Wednesday morning. She had convulsions at the last and was unconscious.

Pa has set out those little peach trees that came up.

The asparagus will be large enough to cut tomorrow.

The Polander over east came

over to have Howard read his card about how much wheat flour he had.

I filled the card out for him. He has a barrel of flour on hand but they say he will not be troubled unless we have 3 or 4 barrels hoarded. I found out what his name is – Frank Copinski.

Ed Smith has bought a cook stove of Woodruff for 4 dollars and has set it up in the shed to cook on this summer and then their kitchen will be cool to eat in. I think it quite an idea.

Mrs. Wrisley has her wrap and it is good and strong, she says she will begin Gladys rug Monday if she feels able. She has been sick the past two weeks. Her back and sides have pained her so she could not work and she did look rather bad.

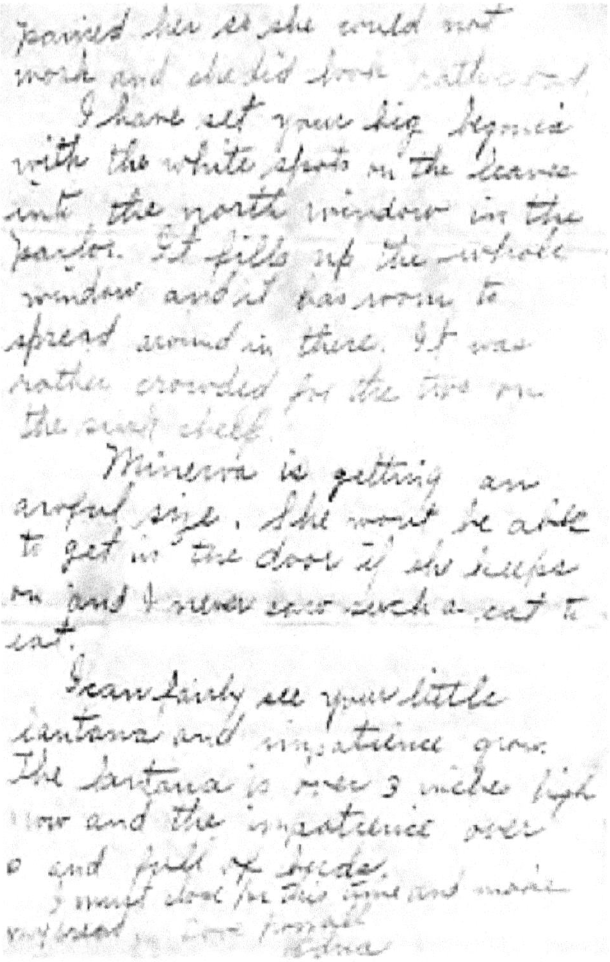

I have set your big begonia with the white spots on the leaves into the north window in the parlor. It fills up the whole window and it has room to spread around in there. It was rather crowded for the two on the sink shelf.

Minerva is getting an awful size. She won't be able to get in the door if she keeps on and I never saw such a cat to eat.

I can fairly see your little lantana and impatience grow. The lantana is over 3 inches high now and the impatience over 6 and full of buds.

I lust close for this time and make my bread.

Love from all,

Edna

The July 4th Letter

Springfield, Vt.

July 6, 1919

Dear Edna,

We are just about half alive after the hot weather. It has been dreadfully warm here so I imagine you have had it too. We had a nice shower this afternoon so probably it will be cooler tomorrow.

We had quite a celebration here the Fourth. There was a fine parade

in the morning. We took Evelyn in her carriage and we all enjoyed it. Some of the floats were as pretty as any

I've ever seen. In the afternoon there was a community picnic up on the fair ground with races, ball game and sports of all kind. We thought it was altogether too warm for Evelyn to go up there so we came home

and had a nap. Toward evening we went up to North Springfield to see the airplane. We saw it go up and land and Lawrence had a chance to see the thing all over so he was right in his glory. I am sending one of the circulars dropped from the plane on the sidewalk in front of the house.

The Kendrick Four Corners is up that road past where Weeden used to live. It is a plane – formerly moving so it's a very suitable place. Mr. Hartness bought it for the town. Everyone was very much interested in the airplane and the pilot took passengers for a dollar a minute. Several went with him – even Mrs. Walter Slack. Yesterday morning he started up and got up fifty feet and struck an air pocket (a place where there is no or very little air) and the thing came down to earth in a hurry. It broke it all to pieces because they are so delicately built; so our amusement is ended till they send another.

We took Mr. Jarvis up to Weathersfield to his brother's farm yesterday morning and went up after him tonight. We took Mrs. Jarvis and the children with us today for a ride. We had a good ride but it rained some.

I got the box of roses yesterday afternoon. They were more wilted than the others were, probably because it was so hot. The buds on the Dorothy Perkins are opening nicely and look quite fresh today.

I suppose I ought to donate the rest of this letter to Evelyn. She is well as can be and doesn't seem to mind the hot weather much. She has been wearing that dress that Lesley made her with the crocheted yoke and she looks so cute in it everyone has to stop and look it over. Her finger is all right and the nail is half grown out. I wish you could see her say "Hello".

A week ago Wednesday Lawrence crushed his middle and fourth fingers dreadfully. An iron bar weighing 100 pounds fell on them and he is losing both nails.

It happened about a quarter of five and when he came home he was as white as a sheet and sick. I soaked them in hot water and then painted them with iodine. They are still very sensitive – but the soreness is nearly gone.

We don't know for sure whether we shall come down home for the vacation week or not but we'll let you know one way of the other before the time comes. Probably we shall come but don't expect us too much.

I must close now as we'll have to get up early tomorrow. We've been lazy for three mornings so it will be hard to get out tomorrow.

Love to all,

Gladys

Glossary
Works Cited
Endnotes
Index

Glossary

ABC

A daily newspaper founded in Madrid, Spain in 1903. Some experts believe it to be the first publication to acknowledge the presence of the Influenza, when the disease made headlines on May 22, 1918. As a result, this is how the strain of Influenza which spawned the 1918 Influenza Epidemic, became known as the "Spanish Flu" or "Spanish Influenza".

Alsace–Lorraine

A hotly contested region of France along the French-German border which the two countries had been fighting over since the mid–16th century, a conflict which intensified following the Franco-Prussian War in 1871. In 1914, Kaiser Wilhelm believed this region to be the gateway to the shortest route to Paris and the westward expansion of the German Empire. The invasion of this region by the German Army via Belgium and the Ardennes on August 4, 1914, is one of several causes which triggered World War One.

Allied Plum Pudding

A steamed plum pudding, which was adapted from the recipe for an English plum pudding commonly eaten at Christmas and was made with raisins, figs, currants and citron. This French take on a classic English recipe was enjoyed by American soldiers who still found themselves stationed in France on Thanksgiving Day 1918, as they waited to be either transferred to Germany and the Allied occupation force or sent home to the United States.

American Influenza

A name, which U.S. Surgeon General Rupert Blue, suggested might become what the strain of flu which spawned the 1918 Influenza Epidemic, would be called, had the virus become too widespread throughout the United States. Fortunately for the American people, this name for the virus was never adopted or widely used.

April 2, 1917

The date on which President Woodrow Wilson went to Congress to ask for a declaration of war on the German Empire, a motion which received unanimous support and passage when it was voted on four days later on April 6th. This move ended the nation's policy on neutrality while also going against Wilson's primary campaign promise of 1916, which was summed up in his 1916 campaign slogan – "He Kept Us (the United States) Out of the War".

The Armistice of Compiegne

The agreement which brought World War One to an official diplomatic end on November 11, 1918 at 11:00am French time or 6:00am Eastern standard time. The Chateau Francfort in the Compiegne Forest was where the German delegation, headed by Matthias Erzberger, was brought from Haudroy, France on the eve of November 7th before being brought to Rethondes, France the next day to commence the negotiations for the Armistice aboard Marshal Ferdinand Foch's personal train.

Armistice Punch

A drink which came about in celebration of the Armistice and was enjoyed by some soldiers on Thanksgiving as well. It's made by dissolving 1½ cups of sugar in 1 cup of hot water. To this, add 1 cup of orange juice and ½ cups of lemon juice. The mixture is then strained over ice and combined with 1 pint each of ginger ale and Lithia; and topped with orange slices and cherries.

Newton D. Baker

The Secretary of War under President Woodrow Wilson during World War One. On July 20, 1917, a blindfolded Baker drew the first Red Ink or Draft number out of a bowl of 10,500 sealed black celluloid capsules, which turned out to be number 258. When a number got selected, every young American man with that number would receive a special green card in the mail about where to go for his draft or pre-service physical, and if passed would then be sent to basic training before going overseas as a soldier.

Big Yellow House

The former home of Walter M. White, a wealthy Springfield (VT) businessman, located at 200 Clinton Street. For three weeks, this building served as a temporary, emergency hospital during the height of the Influenza Epidemic in October 1918, after the main hospital in Springfield ran out of rooms to care for patients.

Rupert Blue

The 4th Surgeon General of the United States, holding that capacity from 1912 to 1920. As Surgeon General, he oversaw the distribution of various pamphlets which at the time were designed to educate the American people about the Influenza virus (H1N1), its impacts, and what measures could be taken to protect oneself from the virus while also keeping it from spreading.

William Bryant & the Chucking Grinder

The founder of Bryant Chucking Grinder Company in 1909 after having been the top draftsman at Jones and Lamson. He founded the company after having, designed and developed the "Chucking Grinder, a grinding machine with three grinding wheels on it, one each for a hole's inside diameter, outside diameter and outside surface. A set-up which made the Chucking Grinder ideal for making artillery and ammunition shells during World War One.

Calling Card

A business-card sized card which in the 19th and early 20th centuries, a young man would drop off at the home of a young woman who he desired to court or in modern terms, take on a date.

Cantigny (France)

A small, French, agricultural village, north of Paris where the American Expeditionary Force (AEF) went on its first offensive action on May 28, 1918 and marked the place where the westward advance of the German Army across Europe was stopped and reversed. This victory would be followed by two more at Chateau-Thierry (June 1st) and Belleau Wood (June 4th).

Charles Lathrop Pack

A wealthy American businessman and philanthropist who organized the National War Garden Commission in March 1917, with the goal of promoting war gardens, small communal or personal gardens which people would use to raise some of their own food. This would then allow American food distributors to direct more of their produce to the soldiers overseas as well as the struggling citizens of Great Britain and France. All this got laid out in his book, *The War Garden Victorious*.

Chow Chow

A variety of pickled relish made by curing green tomatoes and onions in salt overnight. These are then covered with vinegar and cooked slowly for 4 to 5 hours with a spice mixture made up of mustard seed, allspice, cinnamon, ground mustard, black pepper, red pepper (flakes) and brown sugar.

Conscription

A military draft which was implemented by an act of Congress known as the Selective Service Act on May 18, 1917, after it became clear that the United

States military would not grow to the desired size of 10 million men, just through enlistees, or those who volunteered to fight for their country.

Delmonico Salad

Named for the restaurant at which it was introduced, by its head chef, Alessandro Filippini. This salad was a take on the house salad served at Delmonico's Restaurant in New York City. It's a lettuce-based salad, with cheese, eggs, tomatoes and bacon.

The Federal Railroad Administration

One of the four organizations, along with the American Red Cross, the Colgate Company and the United States Post Office, which helped Surgeon General Rupert Blue distribute the pamphlets to the American people which were meant to educate them about the influenza virus and its potential impacts.

"Finis le guerre! Finis le guerre! Vive l'Amerique! Vive la France!"

Translated as, "Finish the war! Finish the war! Long live America! Long live France!", this is the cheer which filled the streets of France, following the announcement of the signing of the Armistice and the end of World War One on November 11, 1918.

Marshal Ferdinand Foch

The French general who served as the Supreme Commander of the Allies during the latter stages of World War One, starting on March 26, 1918. Despite being the top commander of the Allies, he did not have complete control of the American Expeditionary Force, which while part of the Allied Forces, also functioned as a separate fighting entity under the command of General John J. Pershing.

Formitol

One of a couple medications which got prescribed in an attempt to combat the influenza virus. Most of the flu remedies at the time were of the homemade or folk variety and as such, their success was circumstantial and sporadic at best. The drug was originally developed by the E.L. Patch Company and was initially meant to deal with sore throats

Fourteen Points

Principles which President Woodrow Wilson outlined in a speech to Congress on January 8, 1918 regarding what he believed were the goals of the First World War and the terms by which peace was to be negotiated for the war to come to a conclusion. Unfortunately for Wilson, both the American people and a handful of European leaders were somewhat skeptical of the terms laid out in this speech, which also became known as "Wilsonian Idealism" or "Wilsonianism".

Glee Club

A women's choir from Middlebury College, which during World War One and the Influenza Epidemic, went around New England giving concerts in the hopes of providing the local people a happy distraction from the sorrow and misery which dominated many people's lives as a result of the war and the epidemic.

The Great Halifax Explosion

On December 6, 1917, the harbor in Halifax, Nova Scotia, Canada was rocked by a massive explosion, which was caused when two ships; the SS Mont Blanc and the SS Imo collided, setting off the Mont Blanc's dangerous cargo of munitions headed for Europe. Further damage and casualties were avoided thanks to the fast action of Captain Harold Hines and the crew of the USS Old

Colony who quickly sprang into action and set their ship up as a temporary floating hospital.

The Great White Fleet

A popular nickname for the United States Navy in the early years of the 20th century, after a taskforce made up of sixteen battleships and a variety of escort ships, displayed the might and power of the United States Navy by circumnavigating the globe between December 1907 and February 1909.

The Guy Brothers' Minstrels

A minstrel show, known for its blackface routines, which was run by six brothers and originally began in the late 19th century, not long after the American Civil War. Like the Glee Club, the Guy Brothers' Minstrels travelled around, giving performances as a means of providing the American people something to take their minds off World War One and the Influenza Epidemic. The group actually put on a show in Springfield, Vermont on September 2, 1918.

Field Marshal Sir Douglas Haig

The top commander of the British Expeditionary Force (BEF) during World War One.

Warren G. Harding

The 29th president of the United States who finally brought the United States' involvement in World War One to an official conclusion, when he signed into law, the Knox-Porter Resolution on July 2, 1921.

James Hartness

The president and superintendent of the Jones and Lamson Company from 1889 to 1933, who helped three fellow Jones and Lamson employees each start their own machining companies along the Black River in Springfield, Vermont – Edwin Fellows (1896), William Bryant (1909) and Fred Lovejoy (1916). He was also a proponent of war gardens and hiring female machinists during World War One.

The Hindenburg Line

Named for Paul von Hindenburg, commander of the German General Staff from 1916 to 1919, this line of fortifications in Western Belgium was the last line of German defenses before the Belgian-German border. If the Allies could push the German Army back East of the Hindenburg Line, the Germans would be all but forced to surrender. The Allies accomplished this in late September 1918 when they broke through at Cambrai, France.

Hoosac Tunnel

An active railroad tunnel built through the mountains of the Hoosac Range between the Massachusetts towns of Florida and North Adams. A passage

through the mountains had been in existence since the 1820s, with construction on the current tunnel starting in the 1850s. It was also the workers' camp of this project in which Lawrence Reed's biological parents originally met.

Influenza Epidemic

A worldwide flu epidemic which began in 1918 and in some places lasted well into 1919 or even 1920. Both phases of the epidemic became widespread both throughout Western Europe and the United States. The strain of the flu which was responsible for the epidemic was the H1N1 Virus and also came be known as the "Spanish Flu" or "Spanish Influenza".

Isidro Labrador

The patron saint of Madrid, Spain who in the 12th century had the gift of locating previously unknown sources of water in times of need. It was during the Fiesta de San Isidro, a festival in his honor, that the Influenza Epidemic made headlines in the *ABC Newspaper* on May 22, 1918.

January 24, 1923

It was on this day that the last 1,000 American soldiers departed the shores of Europe thus ending the presence of the Allied occupation force in Europe, whose job had been to oversee the rebuilding of Germany and France after the Great War, while ensuring that no further; unprovoked hostilities sprang up along the way, which also came to be known as undesired civil warfare.

Jones and Lamson Company

The first machine company to set up operations in Springfield, Vermont, after local businessman, Adna Brown, promised to buy the majority of its stock if it moved from Windsor, Vermont. The move took place in 1888, after the local townspeople granted the company ten years of tax exempt status by a vote of 534 to 1 on December 3, 1887.

Just a Baby's Prayer at Twilight

Published in 1918 by Waterson, Berlin and Snyder Co., the song was the No. 1 single in the United States that year. The music was composed by M.K. Jerome and the lyrics were written by Sam M. Lewis and Joe Young.

Kaiser Wilhelm II

The leader of the Imperial German Empire from 1888 until he abdicated the throne at the conclusion of World War One in 1918.

King Alfonso XIII

The king of Spain from his birth in 1886 until 1931 when he fled the country in light of a growing sentiment against him, including the loss of the loyalty of the

Spanish military. He did not formally abdicate the throne until 1941, shortly before his passing. He was also one of the more noteworthy individuals to contract the influenza virus during the epidemic in 1918.

The Knox-Porter Resolution

A separate peace treaty between the United States and Germany, which was passed on July 1, 1921 by a special session of Congress, which President Warren Harding had called for the previous April, after the United States refused to ratify and sign the Treaty of Versailles in 1919. The United States' opposition to the Treaty of Versailles stemmed from its opposition to the League of Nations and their differing views on the treaty's reparations settlement. President Harding signed the resolution into law on July 2, 1921.

Liberty Bonds/Liberty Loans

Along with war savings stamps, these were one of the leading ways which the United States used to raise money to fund their war effort. Five separate campaigns to sell these bonds were run during the course of the war, with Springfield being one of the most generous cities in Vermont.

Meatless Days

One of several food consumption measures undertaken by the American people in order to make sure that more of certain foods such as flour and sugar were available to be sent overseas to keep the soldiers both well supplied and well fed.

Meuse-Argonne Offensive

The last major offensive of World War One, which was planned by AEF Colonel George Marshall and embarked on by the American Expeditionary Force with support from French troops on September 26, 1918 with a victory at Somme-Py. This would be followed by victories at Saint-Thierry (Sept. 30), Grand-Pre (Oct. 16) and Montfaucon (Oct. 17) as the AEF surged through the Argonne Forest towards Sedan, France. It was also the final phase of the Hundred Days Offensive.

Moraine

A hill(s) which is formed by a deposit of silt, rock fragments and other materials when the glaciers retreated during the last ice age. The hilly nature of Springfield, Vermont and the waterfalls on the Black River were formed by this type of glacial deposits.

General John J. "Black Jack" Pershing

The commander-in-chief of the American Expeditionary Force during World War One, who insisted that the AEF be allowed to operate as a separate entity while still being part of the Allied Forces. It was the AEF under his command, which helped bring World War One to an end when they captured the railroad station in Sedan, France.

Piave Line

The line of Austrian defenses in Northern Italy, which when broken through by Italian forces, led to the surrender of the Austro-Hungarian forces on November 3, 1918.

Precision Valley

The area along the Black River, including Springfield, Vermont, in which at least a half dozen machine companies set up operations between 1880 and 1920.

Registration Day

June 5, 1917. The date which the Selective Service Act designated to be the day that all American men between the ages of 21 and 30 were to register for a military draft, set to begin on July 20, 1917. Of the 9,586,508 men who registered, 619 came from Springfield, Vermont.

St. Mihiel, France

The last major victory by the American Expeditionary Force over the Germans on September 15, 1918, before the commencement of the Meuse-Argonne Offensive.

Sedan, France

The location of a railroad station along the Carignan-Mezieres Railroad, which was one of two supply and evacuation routes utilized by the German Army. The capture of this station and loss of that route would effectively end Germany's ability to continue fighting. American and French troops captured this station on November 7, 1918 and in turn set in motion the negotiations for the Armistice that evening.

Somewhere in England/Somewhere in France

These are the phrases which American soldiers were told to use when writing home to their family and friends to describe where exactly they were stationed overseas. The need to not use the exact location names was so that if a soldier's letter got intercepted by the Germans, there would be no information inside it which they could use to better plan future attacks on American troops.

Soup to Nuts

A late 19th century expression used to refer to the entirety of something, most commonly a lavish meal such as a 12-course Thanksgiving dinner. The "soup" refers to one of the meal's first courses, while "nuts" refers to one of the meal's final courses.

The Springfield Reporter

The local, weekly newspaper of Springfield, Vermont.

Edgar Sydenstricker

A public health statistician who conducted field studies during the Influenza Epidemic in an effort to determine just how widespread and in what ways, the epidemic was impacting the lives of the American people.

Thanksgiving Proclamation (#1496)

A yearly proclamation issued by President Wilson, which in 1918, he asked the American people to take a couple extra minutes before their meals to honor and remember all of the sacrifices, which they and their fellow Americans had made during the previous 19 months to ensure victory in World War One.

U.S. Chemical Warfare Division

A specialized division of the U.S. Army, whose job it was to penetrate the German Lines and destroy their chemical weapons. Among the more notable members of this division were five future baseball hall-of-famers – Ty Cobb, Christy Mathewson, Branch Rickey, Eppa Rixey and George Sisler.

USS Agamemnon

A German Trans-Atlantic, high-class, high-speed, passenger, ocean liner, which was originally named the SS Kaiser Wilhelm II, when it was built in 1902. It was taken over by the U.S. Government on April 6, 1917 and recommissioned as an American troop transport soon after under the name the USS Kaiser Wilhelm II, which was very quickly changed to the USS Agamemnon.

Veterans Day

What Armistice Day got renamed in 1954 when President Dwight D. Eisenhower in order to ensure that the veterans of all of America's wars get remembered, not just those of World War One.

Voluntary Aid Detachment (V.A.D.)

A unit of female British civilians who volunteered to work in local hospitals providing the necessary nursing care needed by the Allied soldiers who had been injured in France during World War One. Notable members of this unit include British novelist, Agatha Christie; American aviator, Amelia Earhart; and Violet Jessop, who's claim to fame is that she was aboard both the RMS Titanic and the HMHS Britannic when each one sank (1912 and 1916 respectively) as well as the RMS Olympic when it crashed into a British warship in 1911.

War Bread

A brownish, but not overly coarse bread which used only a minimal amount of wheat flour. The reason for the lack of wheat flour in war bread was because the United States Government needed the wheat so that it could be sent overseas to help feed the soldiers in France. It also used molasses as opposed to sugar. For flour, in place of wheat, war bread used a combination of rye flour and cornmeal, two cups of each. A tiny amount of wheat flour was used for kneading only.

Walter Hines Page

The United States ambassador to Great Britain from 1913 to 1918.

Woodrow Wilson

The 28th President of the United States, who held the office from 1913 to 1921 and guided the country through World War One, after winning his second term in 1916 on a campaign promise to keep the nation out of the war.

The Young Women's Mission Club

A women's volunteer organization which constantly aided the American Red Cross back on the homefront, both during and after World War One. Their primary contribution to the war effort was they sewed dresses and other garments which were then sent overseas to be distributed to the many refugee children in the war devastated areas of France, Italy and Poland.

Arthur Zimmerman & the Zimmerman Telegram

The telegram which was written by German Foreign Secretary, Arthur Zimmerman. It was intercepted and deciphered on March 1, 1917 and subsequently appeared in newspapers all across the United States. The telegram detailed how the Germans were preparing to unleash their U-Boats on the American ships which were taking supplies over to Europe in what came to be known as "unrestricted submarine warfare," while also telling of a potential alliance between Germany, Mexico and Japan. Many Americans considered this telegram to be a German declaration of war on the United States.

Works Cited

"3,000,000 Buttons for Fourth Liberty Loan", <u>Springfield Reporter</u>, 26 September 1918: 9.

"A Man's Job", <u>Springfield Reporter</u>, 20 June 1918.

"ABC Newspaper", <u>http://iberianature.com/spain_culture/culture-and-history-of-spain-a/abc-newspaper/</u>

Adwar, Corey. "America Fought Its First D-Day 96 Years Ago Today, And It Was A Huge Success". <u>Business Insider</u>. 22 Dec. 2015. <u>http://www.businessinsider.com/battle-of-st-mihiel-was-americas-first-d-day-2014-9</u>

Alfaro, Danilo, "Consommé: Concentrated Soup Stock", <u>https://www.thespruce.com/what-is-consomme-995766</u>

"American Expeditionary Force at the Battle of Cantigny", <u>http://www.usaww1.com/American-Expeditionary-Force/American-Expeditionary-Force-Battle-of-Cantigny.php4</u>

<u>The Annual Report of the Town Officers of the Town of Springfield, VT for the Year Ending Feb. 1, 1919</u>.

Annual Reprint of the Reports of Council on Pharmacy and Chemistry of the American Medical Association for 1920, Chicago: Press of A.M.A., 1921.

"Armistice Punch Recipe", https://clickamerica.com/recipes/drink-recipes/37-cool-non-alcoholic-drinks-for-an-old-fashioned-punchbowl/

"Arrangement Completed for Red Cross Shipment of Christmas Packages", Springfield Reporter, October 10, 1918: 1.

"At Wilcomb's", Springfield Reporter, 21 November 1918: 5.

Bailey, Beth, "From Front Porch to Back Seat". Magazine of History 18.4 (July 2004): 23-26.

Ball, Ernest R. & J. Keirn Brennan, Good Bye, Good Luck, God Bless You, New York: M. Whitmark & Sons, 1918.

Barney, Keith Richard, The History of Springfield, Vermont: 1885 – 1961, Springfield, VT: Bryant Foundation, 1972.

"Baseball Hall of Fame Veterans" Baseball Almanac, http://www.baseball-almanac.com/hof/veterans_who_are_in_the_hof.shtml

Baskette, Billy & Al Sweet, Each Stitch is a Thought of You, Dear, New York: Leopold Feist, Inc., 1918.

Berry, Leona, Letter to Lawrence Reed, 27 July 1917.

Boyden, George L., If I'm Not At The Roll Call, Kiss Mother Goodbye For Me, New York: Leopold Feist, Inc., 1918.

Brown, Carrie. <u>Rosie's Mom: Forgotten Women Workers of the First World War</u>, Boston: Northeastern University Press, 2002.

Brown, Lew & Albert von Tilzer, <u>I May Be Gone For a Long, Long Time</u>, New York: Broadway Music Corporation, 1917.

Brown, Margaret, Letter to Gladys Reed, 17 February 1918. Brown, Margaret, Letter to Lawrence Reed, 28 November 1915.

Burwell, Sue, "'Light Bearers' Matthew 5:13-16 – June 26, 2016", http:// www. waumc.org/clientimages/53673/6-26-16ser..pdf

"Carl M. Lawrence, Felchville Soldier", <u>Springfield Reporter</u>, 22 November 1917: 7.

Ceresi, Frank, "Chemical Warfare Service: World War One's House of Horrors" <u>Baseball in Wartime</u>, http://www.baseballinwartime.com/chemical_warfare.htm, 2013.

"Chateau Thierry Champagne Pannier NV", http://www.snooth.com/wine/chateau-thierry-champagne-pannier-nv/

"Christmas Packets for Soldiers Abroad", <u>Springfield Reporter</u>, 18 October 1917: 1.

"Claude Barber in France", <u>Springfield Reporter</u>, 24 January 1918.

Clausewitz, Carl von, <u>On War (Vom Kriege)</u>, Ed. Michael Howard & Peter Paret, Princeton, NJ: Princeton University Press, 1976.

Coke, Thomas & Francis Ashbury, <u>The Doctrine and Discipline of the Methodist Episcopal Church in America</u>, Philadelphia: Henry Tuckniss, 1798.

Coleman, Marilyn, Lawrence H. Ganong & Kelly Warzinik. <u>Family Life in 20th Century America</u>, Westport, CT: Greenwood Press, 2007.

Crosby, Alfred W., Jr., <u>Epidemic and Peace, 1918</u>, Westport, CT: Greenwood Press, 1976.

Crowell, Benedict, <u>America's Munitions 1917-1918</u>, Washington, D.C.: GPO, 1919.

Ebor, Donald, <u>The New English Bible</u>, New York: Oxford University Press, 1972.

Ellis, John Tracy, <u>American Catholicism</u>, Chicago: University of Chicago Press, 1956.

"Epidemic Patients Number Nearly 1200", <u>Springfield Reporter</u>, October 17, 1918: 1.

"Every Day: A Thanksgiving Day", <u>Herald and Presbyter</u> 90.47 (19 November 1919): 1.

Filippini, Alessandro, <u>The Delmonico Cook Book</u>, London: Brentano's, 1890.

Fleming, Thomas. <u>The Illusion of Victory: America in World War 1</u>, New York: Basic Books, 2003.

"Food Riot in Bethel", <u>Springfield Reporter</u>, 7 February 1918: 3. "Football in France", <u>Springfield Reporter</u>, 21 February 1918: 1.

Fox, Henry J. & William B. Hoy, <u>Quadrennial Register of the Methodist Episcopal Church and Universal Church Gazetteer, 1852-6</u>, Hartford, CT: Case, Tiffany & Co., 1852.

Freeman. Harold B., <u>The Trail to Home Sweet Home</u>, Providence, RI: Harold Freeman Co., 1918.

Fusonie, Alan E., <u>The Entrepreneurs and the Workers of the Soot: A History of the Foundry in Springfield, Vermont</u>, Woodstock, VT: Anything Printed, 2013.

"G.B. Wilder Writes Home", <u>Springfield Reporter</u>, September 26, 1918: 9.

"Georgia I (Battleship No. 15)", <u>https://www.history.navy.mil/research/histories/ship-histories/danfs/g/georgia-bb-15.html</u>

"Goldenberg's Peanut Chews", <u>http://www.justborn.com/who-we-are/funfacts</u>

Gorley, Bill, Letter to Lawrence Reed, 14 January 1918. Gorley, Bill, Letter to Lawrence Reed, 12 March 1918.

Gurtowski, Richard. "Remembering Baseball Hall of Famers Who Served in the Chemical Corps" <u>Army Chemical Review</u> July-December 2005: 5254.

Hanley, James F. & Ballard Macdonald, <u>Indiana</u>, New York: Shapiro, Bernstein & Co., 1917.

Hanlon, Phyllis. Rev. of. <u>Conscience: Two Soldiers, Two Pacifists, One Family – A Test of Will and Faith in World War 1</u>, by Louisa Thomas. <u>New York Journal of Books</u> 6 June 2011.

Hanson, Captain Joseph Mills, "Those Desperate Days at Chateau-Thierry" <u>The Independent</u> 102.3719 (April 24, 1920): 119+.

"Harding Ends War; Signs Peace Decree at Senator's Home" <u>New York Times</u>, 3 July 1921.

Harris, Charles K., <u>Break the News to Mother</u>, New York: Charles K. Harris, 1897.

Henderson, Mary F., <u>Practical Cooking and Dinner Giving</u>, New York: Harper & Brothers, 1882.

Holmes, R. Derby, <u>A Yankee in the Trenches</u>, Boston: Little, Brown & Co., 1918.

"Hoosac Tunnel History", http://www.hoosactunnel.net/history.php

Horne, Charles F. Ph.D., <u>Source Records of the Great War: Volume II (A.D. 1914)</u>, USA: National Alumni, 1923.

Horne, Charles F. Ph.D., <u>Source Records of the Great War: Volume V (A.D. 1917)</u>, USA: National Alumni, 1923.

Horne, Charles F. Ph.D., <u>Source Records of the Great War: Volume VI</u>

Horne, Charles F. Ph.D., <u>Source Records of the Great War: Volume VII (A.D. 1919)</u>, USA: National Alumni, 1923. http://www.americanprecision.org http://www.eur.army.mil/organization/history.htm

"Influenza 1918", <u>American Experience</u>, PBS.

"Jones & Lamson Co. to Employ Women", <u>Springfield Reporter</u>, 13 December 1917: 1.

Jones, Syd, "Polish Americans", http://www.everyculture.com/multi/Pa-Sp/Polish-Americans.html

Kennedy, David. <u>Over Here: The First World War and American Society</u>, Oxford: Oxford University Press, 2004.

"Kind to French Kiddies", <u>Springfield Reporter</u>, 16 January 1919.

Lewis, Sam M., Joe Young & M.K. Jerome, Just a Baby's Prayer at Twilight (For Her Daddy over There), New York: Waterson, Berlin & Snyder, Co., 1918.

"Live Well in France", Springfield Reporter, 27 December 1917: 1.

Library of Congress, www.loc.gov.

Martin, James, S.J., "The Last Acceptable Prejudice?", <u>America: The Jesuit Review</u> 182.10 (March 25, 2000).

McMaster, John Bach. <u>The United States in the Great War</u>, New York: D. Appleton & Co., 1918.

Merchant, Carrie, Letter to Gladys Reed, 4 February 1918.

"Menu – 1918 Thanksgiving Menu, Camp Hancock, GA"

"Menu – Thanksgiving, November 28, 1918", *Somewhere in France*. "Methodist Church", <u>Springfield Reporter</u>, 26 December 1918: 1.

Miller, James Martin. <u>The People's War Book: History, Cyclopedia and Chronology of the Great World War</u>, Cleveland: R.C. Barnum Co., 1920.

Moore, Helen Watkeys, <u>On Uncle Sam's Water Wagon</u>, New York: G.P. Putnam's Sons, 1919.

"New Year's in France", <u>Springfield Reporter</u>, 31 January 1918: 1. <u>New York Times</u>, 11 November 1918: 1.

"News of the Town: Finis la Guerre", <u>Springfield Reporter</u>, 19 December 1918: 2.

Niese, Joe. <u>Burleigh Grimes: Baseball's Last Legal Spitballer</u>, Jefferson, NC: McFarland, 2013.

O'Hara, Geoffrey, <u>Over Yonder Where the Lilies Grow</u>, New York: Leopold Feist, Inc., 1918.

Ormiston, Rosalind, <u>First World War Posters</u>, London, U.K.: Flame Tree Publishing, 2013.

"Outline of the Terms (Unofficial)", <u>Chicago Daily Tribune</u>, 18 November 1918: 1.

Pack, Charles Lathrop, <u>The War Garden Victorious</u>, Washington, D.C.: National War Garden Commission, 1919.

Pascoe, Richard W., Monte Carlo & Alma M. Sanders, <u>That Tumble-Down Shack in Athlone</u>, New York: Waterson, Berlin & Snyder, Co., 1918.

Pasternak, Suzanne, <u>The Story of the 1917 Halifax Explosion and the Boston Tree</u>, Victoria, B.C.: Friesen Press, 2017.

"Patch's Formitol Tablets", <u>Springfield Reporter</u>, October 10, 1918: 1.

Pershing, John J., <u>Final Report of Gen. John J. Pershing</u>, Washington: GPO, 1920.

Persico, Joseph E., "Little Short of Murder", <u>Military History Quarterly</u> 17.2 (Winter 2005): 26-33.

Picken, Mary Brooks, <u>A Dictionary of Costume and Fashion: Historic and Modern</u>, Mineola, NY: Dover, 1999.

"President Wilson's Declaration of Neutrality", http://wwi.lib.byu.edu/index.php/President_Wilson%27s_Declaration_of_Neutrality

"Priv. Merle S. Whitcomb", <u>Springfield Reporter</u>, 9 January 1919: 3. Putnam, Hugh. Interview, 16 March 2015.

"Quaint People of France", <u>Springfield Reporter</u>, 25 April 1918: 11. "Red Cross Notes", <u>Springfield Reporter</u>, 26 September 1918: 1.

"Red Cross Opened Emergency Hospital", <u>Springfield Reporter</u>, October 10, 1918: 1.

"Rededication of Methodist Church", <u>Springfield Reporter</u>, 12 July 1917.

Redican, Lindsay, "The Forgotten Killer", <u>Influenza Epidemic of 1918</u>, http://www.haverford.edu/biology/edwards/disease/viral_essays/redicanvirus.htm, 1999.

Reed Family Pictures and Documents

Reed, Gladys, Letter to Edna Steere, 6 January 1918.

Reed, Gladys, Letter to Edna Steere, 24 February 1918.

Reed, Gladys, Letter to Edna Steere, 17 June 1918.

Reed, Gladys, Letter to Edna Steere, 17 September 1918.

Reed, Gladys, Letter to Edna Steere, 25 September 1918.

Reed, Gladys, Letter to Edna Steere, 2 October 1918.

Reed, Gladys, Letter to Edna Steere, 7 October 1918.

Reed, Gladys, Letter to Edna Steere, 13 October 1918.

Reed, Gladys, Letter to Edna Steere, 21 October 1918.

Reed, Gladys, Letter to Edna Steere, 10 November 1918.

Reed, Gladys, Letter to Edna Steere, 15 November 1918.

Reed, Gladys, Letter to Edna Steere, 17 November 1918.

Reed, Gladys, Letter to Edna Steere, 15 December 1918.

Reed, Gladys, Letter to Edna Steere, 22 December 1918.

Reed, Gladys, Letter to Edna Steere, 29 December 1918.

Reed, Gladys, Letter to Edna Steere, 9 February 1919.

Reed, Gladys, Letter to Edna Steere, 15 February 1919.

Reed, Gladys, Letter to Edna Steere, 23 February 1919.

Reed, Gladys, Letter to Edna Steere, 25 February 1919.

Reed, Gladys, Letter to Edna Steere, 16 March 1919.

Reed, Gladys, Letter to Edna Steere, 8 June 1919.

Reed, Gladys, Letter to Edna Steere, 22 June 1919.

Reed, Gladys, Letter to Edna Steere, 29 June 1919.

Reed, Gladys, Letter to Edna Steere, 29 September 1919.

Reed, Lawrence, Letter to Gladys Reed, 5 June 1917.

Reed, Lawrence, Letter to Gladys Reed, 17 June 1917.

Reed, Lawrence, Letter to Gladys Steere, 30 April 1915.

Reed, Lawrence, Letter to Gladys Steere, 8 May 1915.

Reed, Lawrence, Letter to Gladys Steere, 28 July 1915.

Reed, Lawrence, Letter to Gladys Steere, 8 August 1915.

Reed, Lawrence, Letter to Gladys Steere, 16 August 1915.

Reed, Lawrence, Letter to Gladys Steere, 8 January 1916.

Reed, Lawrence, Letter to Gladys Steere, 23 January 1916.

Reed, Lawrence, Letter to Gladys Steere, 8 April 1917.

Reed, Lawrence, Letter to Gladys Steere, 12 April 1917.

Reed, Lawrence, Letter to Gladys Steere, 29 April 1917.

Reed, Lawrence, Letter to Gladys Steere, 15 May 1917.

"Resumen de Noticias", <u>ABC (Madrid)</u>, 22 May 1918: 24.

Rhodes, Frank H.T., <u>Geology</u>, New York: Golden Books, 1991.

"Roy G. Faxon Spins a Sailor's Yarn", <u>Springfield Reporter</u>, 2 January 1919: 2.

Scanlon, Joseph, "Source of Threat and Source of Assistance: The Maritime Aspects of the 1917 Halifax Explosion" <u>The Northern Mariner</u> 10.4 (October 2000): 39-50.

Schuffman, Lawrence D., "'Capitalizing on American Pride and Patriotism: Funding of the First World War through The Liberty and Victory Loan Bonds, 1917-1923" <u>Paper Money</u> 48.1 (January/February 2009): 3-33.

Seib, Philip, <u>The Player: Christy Mathewson, Baseball and the American Century</u>, New York: Avalon, 2003.

"Sergt. C.P. Bacon. Right at the Front", <u>Springfield Reporter</u>, 18 July 1918: 5.

"Service Flag of Twenty-Three Stars", <u>Springfield Reporter</u>, 21 February 1918: 1.

Shannon, J.R. & A.J. Stasny, <u>Rose Dreams</u>, New York: A.J. Stasny Music Co., 1918.

"Soldier's Letter", <u>Springfield Reporter</u>, 25 July 1918: 3.

"Soldiers' Letters", <u>Springfield Reporter</u>, 11 April 1918: 7.

"Soldiers' Letters", <u>Springfield Reporter</u>, 16 May 1918: 7.

"Soldiers' Letters", <u>Springfield Reporter</u>, 4 July 1918: 7.

"Soldiers' Letters", <u>Springfield Reporter</u>, 8 August 1918: 5.

"Soldiers' Letters", <u>Springfield Reporter</u>, 15 August 1918: 5.

"Soldiers' Letters", <u>Springfield Reporter</u>, 22 August 1918: 7.

"Soldiers' Letters from Camp in France", <u>Springfield Reporter</u>, 6 December 1917: 2.

<u>Springfield Reporter</u>, 3 April 1917.

<u>Springfield Reporter</u>, 13 April 1917.

<u>Springfield Reporter</u>, 27 April 1917.

<u>Springfield Reporter</u>, 4 May 1917.

<u>Springfield Reporter</u>, 11 May 1917.

<u>Springfield Reporter</u>, 18 May 1917.

<u>Springfield Reporter</u>, 25 May 1917.

<u>Springfield Reporter</u>, 1 June 1917.

<u>Springfield Reporter</u>, 8 June 1917.

<u>Springfield Reporter</u>, 14 June 1917.

Springfield Reporter, 21 June 1917.

Springfield Reporter, 5 July 1917.

Springfield Reporter, 27 September 1917.

Springfield Reporter, 11 October 1917.

Springfield Reporter, 18 October 1917.

Springfield Reporter, 27 December 1917.

Springfield Reporter, 10 January 1918.

Springfield Reporter, 4 April 1918.

Springfield Reporter, 18 April 1918.

Springfield Reporter, 20 June 1918.

Springfield Reporter, 26 September 1918.

Springfield Reporter, 3 October 1918.

Springfield Reporter, 10 October 1918.

Springfield Arts and Historical Society.

"Springfield's Honor Roll", Springfield Reporter, 27 December 1917: 3.

"Steamed Plum Pudding", <u>New England Today</u>, https://newengland.com/today/food/desserts/puddings-custards/steamed-plum-pudding/

Stead, Alfred, "'Tommy Atkins' in the Trenches" <u>The Independent</u> 80.3439 (November 9, 1914): 197-200.

Steere, Edna, Letter to Della Steere, 24 August 1919.

Steere, Edna, Letter to Della Steere, 7 September 1919.

Steere, Edna, Letter to Della Steere, 14 September 1919.

Steere, Gladys, Letter to Lawrence Reed, 29 August 1915.

Steere, Gladys, Letter to Lawrence Reed, 7 November 1915.

Steere, Gladys, Letter to Lawrence Reed, 10 April 1917.

Steere, Gladys, Letter to Lawrence Reed, 15 April 1917.

Steere, Gladys, Letter to Lawrence Reed, 24 April 1917.

<u>Still Another: A Book of Choice Recipes</u> 2nd Edition, Oakland, CA: Tribune Publishing, 1883.

Stubbs, Kevin D., <u>Race to the Front</u>, Westport, CT, Praeger Publishers: 2002

"Supplies to Militia", <u>Springfield Reporter</u>, 5 July 1917.

Sydenstricker, Edgar, "Preliminary Statistics of the Influenza Epidemic", <u>Public Health Reports</u> 33.52 (Dec. 27, 1918): 2305-2321.

Terraine, John, The Great War, Ware, Great Britain: Wordsworth, 1997.

"Thanksgiving Day Dinner Menu – November 28, 1918", *Second Aviation Instruction Center.*

"Thanksgiving Day – USS Wilmington – November 28, 1918".

"Thanksgiving Dinner – November 28, 1918", *26th Machine Gun Battalion, Company B – Camp Sheridan, Alabama.*

"Thanksgiving Dinner – November 28, 1918", *Naval Torpedo Station – Newport, RI.*

"Thanksgiving Menu", *Camp Funston, KS.*

"Thanksgiving Menu – November 28, 1918", *Naval Ammunition Depot, Fort Mifflin, PA.*

"Thanksgiving Menu – Thanksgiving Day 1918", *USS Agamemnon.*

"Thanksgiving Menu – Thursday, November 28, 1918", *USS Georgia.*

"Thanksgiving Proclamation", Chicago Daily Tribune, 18 November 1918: 17.

Thigpen, Susan, The Mountain Laurel Cookbook, USA: CreateSpace, 2015.

Trilla, Antoni, Guillem Trilla & Carolyn Daer, "The 1918 'Spanish Flu' in Spain", Clinical Infectious Diseases 47.5 (September 1, 2008): 668-73.

"Uncle Sam's Advice on Flu", <u>Springfield Reporter</u>, October 17, 1918.

<u>United States Army in the World War 1917-1919: Volume 16 (General Orders, GHQ, AEF)</u>, Washington, D.C.: U.S. Government Printing Office, 1948.

United States Geologic Survey.

"USS Manley", http://destroyerhistory.org/flushdeck/ussmanley/

"W.H. Wheeler and Son: Gift Suggestions", <u>Springfield Reporter</u>, 12 December 1918: 4.

"War Bread or Thirds Bread", <u>WW1 Bread Recipes</u>, http://dwittopinions.wordpress.com/2013/12/27/wwi-bread-recipes/

Wilson, Woodrow, "Fourteen Points" <u>Avalon Project</u>, http://avalon.law.yale.edu/20th_century/wilson14.asp

Wilson, Woodrow, "Proclamation 1496 – Thanksgiving Day 1918", <u>The American Presidency Project</u>, http://www.presidency.ucsb.edu/ ws/?pid=72444

Wilson, Woodrow, "Today is Armistice Day", <u>Mt. Sterling Advocate</u> 29.20 (November 11, 1919).

Yoder, Anne."Military Classifications for Draftees" http://www.swarthmore.edu/library/peace/conscientiousobjection/MilitaryClassifications.htm

Endnotes

1   Hugh Putnam, Interview, March 16, 2015.

2   Charles F. Horne, Source Records of the Great War: Volume II (A.D. 1914) (USA: National Alumni, 1923): xx.

3   "President Wilson's Declaration of Neutrality": 1.

4   Charles F. Horne, Source Records of the Great War: Volume V (A.D. 1917) (USA: National Alumni, 1923): 126.

5   Ibid., 137.

6   Ibid., xxiii.

7   Ibid.

8   "Hoosac Tunnel History": 1-2.

9   Margaret Brown, Letter to Lawrence Reed, 28 November 1915.

10 Beth Bailey, "From Front Porch to Back Seat: A History of the Date", Magazine of History 18.4 (July 2004): 25.

11 Ibid.

12 Marilyn Coleman, Family Life in 20th Century America (Westport, CT: Greenwood Press, 2007): 3.

13 Ibid.

14 Ibid., 4.

15 Ibid.

16 Ibid., 4-5.

17 Ibid., 6.

18   Lawrence Reed, Letter to Gladys Steere, 8 August 1915.

19   Gladys Steere, Letter to Lawrence Reed, 29 August 1915.

20   Lawrence Reed, Letter to Gladys Steere, 16 August 1915.

21   Ibid., 28 July 1915.

22   Gladys Steere, Letter to Lawrence Reed, 7 November 1915.

23   Lawrence Reed, Letter to Gladys Steere, 8 May 1915.

24   Ibid., 23 January 1916.

25   Ibid., 8 January 1916.

26   Ibid., 15 May 1917.

27   Ibid., 30 April 1915.

28   Ibid., 8 April 1917.

29   Gladys Steere, Letter to Lawrence Reed, 10 April 1917.

30   Lawrence Reed, Letter to Gladys Steere, 8 April 1917.

31   Source Records: Volume V, 183.

32   Lawrence Reed, Letter to Gladys Steere, 12 April 1917.

33   Ibid.

34   Gladys Steere, Letter to Lawrence Reed, 15 April 1917.

35   Lawrence Reed, Letter to Gladys Steere, 29 April 1917.

36   Ibid., 15 May 1917.

37   Lawrence Reed, Letter to Gladys Reed, 5 June 1917.

38   Keith Richard Barney, The History of Springfield, Vermont: 18851961 (Springfield, VT, Bryant, 1972): 175.

39   Anne Yoder, "Military Classifications for Draftees": 1.

40   Charles Lathrop Pack, The War Garden Victorious (Washington, D.C., War Garden Comm., 1919): 12.

41   The History of Springfield, Vermont: 1885-1961, 174.

42   Ibid.

43   Ibid.

44   "Supplies to Militia", Springfield Reporter, 5 July 1917: 1.

45   "Jones & Lamson Co. to Employ Women" Springfield Reporter, 13 December 1917: 1.

46   Carrie Brown, Rosie's Mom (Boston, Northeastern University Press, 2002): 136-42.

47   Source Records: Volume V, xxii.

48   Ibid., xxii-xxiii.

49   "Springfield's Honor Roll", Springfield Reporter, 27 December 1917: 3.

50   "Christmas Packets for Soldiers Abroad", Springfield Reporter, 18 October 1917: 1.

51   Ibid.

52   Source Records: Volume V, 429.

53   Leona Berry, Letter to Lawrence Reed, 27 July 1917.

54   "Carl M. Lawrence, Felchville Soldier", Springfield Reporter 22 November 1917: 7.

55   Ibid.

56   Ibid.

57   "Soldiers' Letters From Camp in France", Springfield Reporter, 6 December 1917: 2.

58   United States Army in the World War 1917-1919: Volume 16 (General Orders, GHQ, AEF), (Washington, D.C.: U.S. Government Printing Office, 1948): 3.

59   Ibid., 4.

60   Ibid., 5.

61   Ibid., 6.

62   Ibid.

63   Ibid.

64   Soldiers' Letters From Camp in France", Springfield Reporter, 6
      December 1917: 2.

65   Source Records: Volume V

66   "Live Well in France", Springfield Reporter, 27 December 1917: 1.

67   Ibid.

68   Gladys Reed, Letter to Edna Steere, 6 January 1918.

69   "Food Riot in Bethel", Springfield Reporter, 7 February 1918: 3.

70   Carrie Merchant, Letter to Gladys Reed, 4 February 1918.

71   Margaret Brown, Letter to Gladys Reed, 17 February 1918.

72   Ibid.

73   Gladys Reed, Letter to Edna Steere, 24 February 1918.

74   Ibid.

75   Bill Gorley, Letter to Lawrence Reed, 14 January 1918.

76   "Service Flag of Twenty-Three Stars", Springfield Reporter, 21 Febru-
      ary 1918: 1.

77   Bill Gorley, Letter to Lawrence Reed, 12 March 1918.

78   "New Year's in France", Springfield Reporter, 31 January 1918: 1.

79   Ibid.

80   "Claude Barber in France", Springfield Reporter, 24 January 1918.

81   "Football in France", Springfield Reporter, 21 February 1918: 1.

82   "Soldiers' Letters", Springfield Reporter, 11 April 1918: 7.

83   Ibid.

84   "Quaint People of France", Springfield Reporter, 25 April 1918: 11.

85   Alfred Stead, "Tommy Atkins' in the Trenches", The Independent

80.3439 (November 9, 1914): 197.

86   Ibid.

87   Ibid.

88   Ibid., 198.

89   "Soldiers' Letters", Springfield Reporter, 16 May 1918: 7.

90   "American Expeditionary Force at the Battle of Cantigny": 1.

91   Ibid., 1-2.

92   Ibid., 3.

93   "Soldiers' Letters", Springfield Reporter, 4 July 1918: 7.

94   Ibid.

95   Ibid.

96   Captain Joseph Mills Hanson, "Those Desperate Days at Chateau-Thierry", The Independent 102.3719 (April 24, 1920): 120.

97   "Sergt. C. P. Bacon, Right at the Front", Springfield Reporter, 18 July 1918: 5.

98   "A Man's Job", Springfield Reporter, 20 June 1918.

99   "Soldier's Letter", Springfield Reporter, 25 July 1918: 3.

100   Ibid.

101   Ibid., 287.

102   Joseph E. Persico, "Little Short of Murder", Military History Quarterly 17.2 (Winter 2005): 26.

103   James Martin Miller, The People's War Book (Cleveland: R.C. Barnum Co., 1920).

104   Gladys Reed, Letter to Edna Steere, November 10, 1918

105   Source Records: Volume VI, 354.

106   "Outline of the Terms (Unofficial)", Chicago Daily Tribune, 18 November 1918: 1.

107   New York Times, 11 November 1918: 1.

108   Ibid.

109   Ibid.

110   Ibid.

111   Ibid.

112   Charles F. Horne, Source Records of the Great War: Volume VII (A.D. 1919),(USA: National Alumni, 1923): 153.

113   Ibid., 189.

114   "Harding Ends War; Signs Peace Decree at Senator's Home" New York Times, 3 July 1921.

115   Source Records: Volume VII, 189.

116   Gladys Reed, Letter to Edna Steere, November 10, 1918

117   Ibid., November 17, 1918.

118   Ibid.

119   Ibid.

120   "Thanksgiving Proclamation", Chicago Daily Tribune, 18 November 1918: 17.

121   Woodrow Wilson, "Proclamation 1496 – Thanksgiving Day 1918", The American Presidency Project.

122   Source Records: Volume VI, 431-32.

123   Henry J. Fox & William B. Hoyt, Quadrennial Register of the Methodist Episcopal Church and Universal Church Gazetteer, 1852-6 (Hartford, CT: Case, Tiffany & Co., 1852): 297.

124   The Doctrines and Discipline of the Methodist Episcopal Church in America, 171

125   Thomas Coke & Francis Ashbury, The Doctrines and Discipline of the Methodist Episcopal Church in America (Philadelphia: Henry Tuckniss, 1798): 150.

126   "Resumen de Noticias", ABC (Madrid), 22 May 1918: 24.

127   Lindsay Redican, "The Forgotten Killer", Influenza Epidemic of 1918: 1.

128   Alfred W. Crosby, Jr., Epidemic and Peace, 1918 (Westport, CT: Greenwood Press, 1976): 37.

129   "The Forgotten Killer", 2.

130   Ibid.

131   Ibid., 1.

132   Ibid., 1-2 (Crosby 21).

133   Ibid., 2 (Crosby 26).

134   Ibid., 2.

135   Ibid.

136   Ibid.

137   Ibid.

138   Ibid., 2 (Crosby 49).

139   "Red Cross Notes", Springfield Reporter, 26 September 1918: 1.

140   Gladys Reed, Letter to Edna Steere, October 2, 1918.

141   Ibid., September 17, 1918.

142   http://www.flu.gov/pandemic/history/1918/the_pandemic/fightingin-fluenza/

143   Ibid.

144   Gladys Reed, Letter to Edna Steere, September 25, 1918.

145   Ibid., October 2, 1918.

146   Ibid.

147   Ibid., October 7, 1918.

148   Ibid.

149   Alan E. Fusonie, The Entrepreneurs and the Workers of the Soot (Woodstock, VT: Anything Printed, 2013): 86-87.

150   Ibid.

151   Gladys Reed, Letter to Edna Steere, October 7, 1918.

152   Ibid.

153   Ibid.

154   "Influenza 1918", American Experience, PBS.

155   Ibid.

156   Ibid.

157   Gladys Reed, Letter to Edna Steere, October 13, 1918.

158   "Influenza 1918", American Experience, PBS.

159   Ibid.

160   Ibid.

161   Ibid.

162   Ibid.

163   Annual Reprint of the Reports of Council on Pharmacy and Chemistry of the A.M.A. (Chicago: Press of A.M.A., 1921): 21-23.

164   Ibid.

165   "Patch's Formitol Tablets", Springfield Reporter, October 10, 1918:1.

166   "Red Cross Opened Emergency Hospital", Springfield Reporter, October 10, 1918: 1.

167   "Epidemic Patients Number Nearly 1200", Springfield Reporter , October 17, 1918: 1.

168   Gladys Reed, Letter to Edna Steere, October 13, 1918.

169   Ibid., October 21, 1918.

170   Antoni Trilla, "The 1918 'Spanish Flu' in Spain", Clinical Infectious Diseases 47.5 (September 1, 2008): 668-69.

171   Ibid.

172   Ibid.

173   Ibid.

174   "Epidemic Patients Nearly 1200", Springfield Reporter, October 17, 1918: 1.

175   "Uncle Sam's Advice on Flu", Springfield Reporter, October 17, 1918.

176   Ibid.

177   Ibid.

178   Gladys Reed, Letter to Edna Steere, October 21, 1918.

179   Ibid., March 16, 1919.

180   "Uncle Sam's Advice on Flu", Springfield Reporter, October 17,1918.

181   Ibid.

182   Ibid.

183   Gladys Reed, Letter to Edna Steere, October 13, 1918.

184   Ibid., October 21, 1918.

185   Ibid.

186   "Uncle Sam's Advice on Flu", Springfield Reporter, October 17, 1918.

187   Keith Richard Barney, The History of Springfield, Vermont: 18851961 (Springfield, VT, Bryant, 1972): 181.

188   Ibid.

189   Ibid.

190   Ibid.

191   Edgar Sydenstricker, "Preliminary Statistics of the Influenza Epidemic", Public Health Reports 33.52 (Dec. 27, 1918): 2319.

192   Ibid.

193   "Soldiers' Letters", Springfield Reporter, August 8, 1918: 5.

194   Ibid.

195   "Soldiers' Letters", Springfield Reporter, August 15, 1918: 5.

196   "Soldiers' Letters", Springfield Reporter, August 22, 1918: 7.

197   "G.B. Wilder Writes Home", Springfield Reporter, September 26, 1918: 9.

198   "3,000,000 Buttons for Fourth Liberty Loan", Springfield Reporter, September 26, 1918: 9.

199   "Arrangement Completed for Red Cross Shipment of Christmas Packages", Springfield Reporter, October 10, 1918: 1.

200   Ibid.

201   Gladys Reed, Letter to Edna Steere, October 7, 1918.

202   Edgar Sydenstricker, "Preliminary Statistics of the Influenza Epidemic", Public Health Reports 33.52 (Dec. 27, 1918).

203   Ibid.

204   Ibid.

205   Source Records: Volume VI: 354.

206   Kevin D. Stubbs, Race to the Front (Westport, CT: Praeger, 2002): 262.

207   Source Records: Volume VI: 398-99.

208   Ibid., 399.

209   Ibid., 399-400.

210   Alessandro Filippini, The Delmonico Cook Book (London: Brenta-no's, 1890): 314.

211   "Georgia I (Battleship No. 15)", https://www.history.navy.mil/research/histories/ship-histories/danfs/g/georgia-bb-15.html

212   Ibid.

213   Danilo Alfaro, "Consommé: Concentrated Soup Stock", https://www.thespruce.com/what-is-consomme-995766

214   Benedict Crowell, America's Munitions 1917-1918 (Washington, D.C.: GPO, 1919): 449.

215   Ibid.

216   "Goldenberg's Peanut Chews", http://www.justborn.com/who-weare/fun-facts

217   Benedict Crowell, America's Munitions 1917-1918 (Washington, D.C.: GPO, 1919): 449.

218   "Goldenberg's Peanut Chews", http://www.justborn.com/who-weare/fun-facts

219   "Chateau Thierry Champagne Pannier NV", http://www.snooth.com/wine/chateau-thierry-champagne-pannier-nv/

220   Helen Watkeys Moore, On Uncle Sam's Water Wagon (New York: G.P. Putnam's Sons, 1919): 152.

221   Susan Thigpen, The Mountain Laurel Cookbook (USA: CreateSpace, 2015).

222   Source Records: Volume VI.

223   http://www.eur.army.mil/organization/history.htm

224   Gladys Reed, Letter to Edna Steere, December 15, 1918.

225   Ibid., November 15, 1918.

226   "At Wilcomb's", Springfield Reporter, November 21, 1918: 5.

227   "W.H. Wheeler and Son: Gift Suggestions", Springfield Reporter, December 12, 1918: 4.

228   Ibid.

229   Ibid.

230   "News of the Town: Finis la Guerre", Springfield Reporter, December 19, 1918: 2.

231   Ibid.

232   Gladys Reed, Letter to Edna Steere, December 22, 1918.

233   Ibid.

234   Gladys Reed, Letter to Della Steere, December 29, 1918

236   Ibid.

237   Mary Brooks Picken, A Dictionary of Costume and Fashion: Historic and Modern (Mineola, NY: Dover, 1999): 71.

238   Ibid., 24.

239   Ibid., 47.

240   Ibid.

241   "Methodist Church", Springfield Reporter, December 26, 1918: 1.

242   "Roy G. Faxon Spins a Sailor's Yarn", Springfield Reporter, January 2, 1919: 2.

243   "USS Manley", http://destroyerhistory.org/flushdeck/ussmanley/

244   "Roy G. Faxon Spins a Sailor's Yarn", Springfield Reporter, January 2, 1919: 2.

245   "Priv. Merle S. Whitcomb", Springfield Reporter, January 9, 1919: 3.

246   Ibid.

247   "Kind to French Kiddies", Springfield Reporter, January 16, 1919.

248   Gladys Reed, Letter to Edna Steere, February 9, 1919.

249   Ibid., February 15, 1919.

250   Ibid., February 23, 1919.

251   Ibid., February 25, 1919.

252   Ibid., March 16, 1919.

253   Ibid., June 8, 1919.

254   Ibid., June 22, 1919.

255   Ibid., June 29, 1919.

256   James Martin, S.J., "The Last Acceptable Prejudice?", America: The Jesuit Review 182.10 (March 25, 2000).

257   Edna Steere, Letter to Della Steere, August 24, 1919.

258   Ibid., September 7, 1919.

259   Ibid., September 14, 1919.

260   Gladys Reed, Letter to Edna Steere, September 29, 1919.

261   Woodrow Wilson, "Today is Armistice Day", Mt. Sterling Advocate 29.20 (November 11, 1919).

262   Ibid.

Index